REAL MEN DO EAT QUICHE!

HEARTY, HEALTHY RECIPES FOR THE MAN IN YOUR LIFE

REAL MEN DO EAT QUICHE!

REAL MEN DO EAT QUICHE!

FIONA SMITH

HEARTY, HEALTHY RECIPES FOR THE MAN
IN YOUR LIFE

LifeStyle

By Fiona Smith
Photography by Tine Drost

This edition first published in Great Britain in 1999 by
LifeStyle
An imprint of Parkgate Books
Kiln House, 210 New Kings Road, London SW6 4NZ

© 1999 Parkgate Books

A CIP catalogue record for this book is available from the
British Library.

ISBN 1-902617-03-7

Printed and bound in Hong Kong

FISH   **8**
Fish & Chips   9
Fish Cakes   10
Fish Stew   11
Fisherman's Pie   12
Tuna & Cannellini Bean Salad   12
Lemon & Basil Salmon with Pesto Mash   13
Lemon-Crusted Cod with Five-Minute Ratatouille   14
Moroccan Fish Soup   15
Mussels with Black Bean Sauce   16
Quick Fish Curry   17
Salade Niçoise Stuffed Loaf   18
Seafood Gumbo   19
Smoked Haddock Crêpes   20
Smoked Mackerel Hash   21
Smoked Mackerel Kedgeree   22
Sole with Tomato & Cinnamon   23
Squid Salad with Lime Dressing   24
Sweet & Sour Fish   25

PASTA   **26**
Cannelloni with Beans & Herbs   27
Artichoke, Walnut & Mushroom Pizza   28
Fresh Tomato Sauce   29
Farfalle with Smoked Chicken   30
Parsnip & Carrot Frittata   31
Mexican-Style Pasta   32
Penne with Green Beans & Walnut Sauce   33
Pasta Ribbons with Cottage Cheese & Greens   34
Pumpkin Gnocchi with Spinach   35
Potato & Rosemary Focaccia   36
Spaghetti Bake   37
Pumpkin, Sweet Potato & Orange Pasta   38
Tomato & Tuna Pasta   39
Spinach & Mushroom Lasagne   40
Vegetable Stir-fry with Peanut Noodles   41
Vegetable & Feta Cheese Calzone   42
Winter Vegetable Calzone   43

POULTRY	**44**
Baked Chicken with Carrot & Onion	45
Avocado & Chicken Caesar Salad	46
Chicken Crumble	47
Chicken Burritos	48
Chicken with Apricots & Almonds	49
Chicken Noodle Salad	50
Chilli Chicken with Water Chestnuts	51
Chicken with Asparagus	52
Greek Chicken & Lemon Soup	53
Easy Peking-Style Chicken	54
One-Pot Chicken with Rice	55
Tandoori Chicken	56
Turkey Chow Mein	56
Nut Stuffing for Chicken	57
Quick Coq au Vin	58
Turkey Korma with Beans	59

PULSES	**60**
Aubergine Houmous	61
Beans & Rice	62
Butter & Broad Bean Soup	63
Corn & Sweet Potato Soup with Beans	64
Cottage Pie	65
Falafel Patties	66
Moroccan-Style Chickpeas with Lamb	67
Pasta & Bean Soup	68
Pea & Avocado Guacamole	69
Re-Fried Bean Tacos	70
Spicy Black-Eyed Bean Dip	71
Spicy Cauliflower with Lentils & Rice	72
Spicy Chickpea Pockets	73
Spicy Lentil Soup	74
Vegetable Burgers	75

RICE	**76**
Baked Mushrooms with Brown Rice & Spinach	77
Cabbage, Potato & Rice Soup	78
Nutty Pilau Rice	78
Fried Rice	79
Vegetable Rice with Eggs	80
Pea & Ham Risotto	81
Thai Sweet Potato & Spinach Curry	82
Three-Grain Tabouleh	83

VEGETABLES	**84**
Gazpacho	85
Carrot, Mushroom & Nut Loaf	86
Mushroom & Walnut Stroganoff	87
Greek Stuffed Peppers	88
Spicy Tofu with Corn	89
Roast Vegetable Salad	90
Vegetable Kebabs with Halloumi Cheese	91
Tofu with Broccoli & Pork	92
Watercress & Spinach Soup with Almonds	93

REAL MEN DO EAT QUICHE!

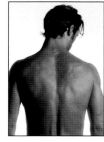

REAL MEN DO EAT

WOULD YOU like to eat a lower-fat diet, in order to lose a few pounds or simply to be healthier, but are put off by the howls of disgust from your partner, or the whole family when you present them with a tiny portion of a ready-made meal? If so, this book is for you.

Real Men Do Eat Quiche! shows you how to prepare balanced and varied meals that are low in fat but high in taste. Some of the recipes are new twists on old favourites, others are taken from around the world and will add some spice to your life! Together they aim to provide you with all the protein, carbohydrates, fibre, vitamins and minerals necessary to your well-being.

There are sections on five of the main staples in a healthy diet – fish, pasta, poultry, pulses and rice – as well as one dealing with hard-core vegetable dishes. Most of the recipes in this book use lots of vegetables, but for those that don't it is important to include vegetables as a side dish.

Real Men Do Eat Quiche! is designed to show that red meat does not have to be the beginning and end of your repertoire. The six sections of this book demonstrate the variety and balance that can be achieved with hardly a glance at the beef, lamb and pork shelves of the supermarket. However, if you do decide to include red meat in your meal, choose lean cuts, or trim off all the fat, and use a cooking method that doesn't require excess additional fat, such as grilling or stir-frying. When additional fats are needed, stay away from animal fats and stick to oils.

QUICHE!

One of the best and healthiest oils is olive, which gives a tangy Mediterranean flavour to your food. Try groundnut oil for a nutty eastern flavour, and rape seed or sunflower for a neutral taste when other flavours in the recipe are strong. A small amount of oil in your diet is not bad, and will add flavour to your cooking.

Most of the recipes here are very easy indeed, and are marked with one asterisk (★). Two asterisks (★★) means it's slightly less easy, and a few, with three asterisks (★★★), need a bit more concentration.

Fish is a wonderful protein-packed food. Most kinds of fish are low in fat, but even the high-fat fish, such as salmon and mackerel, are full of essential fatty acids that we require for healthy living. Seafood is also full of goodness, but beware — it has a reputation for promoting lustful thoughts!

When choosing your fish, you should go for the freshest available. This is why, in most recipes, I have only given suggestions of the type of fish you might like to use.

FISH & CHIPS

Fish & Chips that go nowhere near a deep-fat fryer. Not as easy as going down to the chip shop, but a lot tastier and less greasy.

SERVES 2
1 hour
★★

INGREDIENTS:

- 4 medium potatoes, scrubbed and cut into thick wedges
- 2 tbsp olive oil
- 1 tbsp mild paprika
- 2 tsp salt
- 4 large or 8 small sheets of filo pastry
- 2 x 150–200g/5–6½oz fillets of cod or haddock
- lemon wedges to serve
- vinegar, ketchup, pickled onions, gherkins (optional)
- salt and pepper

METHOD:

Preheat the oven to 200°C/400°F/Gas Mark 6. Bring the potatoes to the boil in salted water and then drain, covering with a tea towel to dry out. Combine them with the paprika, half the oil and some salt in a roasting dish. Bake for 40 minutes. Lay out 1 large or 2 small sheets of filo and brush with oil. Place another sheet on top and place a piece of fish at one end, season with salt and pepper, and roll up, folding in the sides. Brush the top with oil. Repeat with the other filo and fish. Bake for 15 minutes. Serve with lemon wedges and condiments of choice.

FISH CAKES

These fish cakes make a great party food, or a meal. The dipping sauce is a sweet and sour type, but you could use hoisin, chilli or another sauce of choice. The basic fish cake mixture can be spiced up with 1 tsp of five-spice powder, and some chopped chilli, or chilli sauce.

SERVES 2
20 minutes
★★

INGREDIENTS:

- *330g/11oz fish fillet (e.g. salmon, cod, snapper), minced*
- *6 spring onions, finely sliced*
- *150g/5oz mashed potato*
- *85g/3oz baby corn, finely sliced*
- *75g/2½oz green beans, finely sliced*
- *salt and white or Szechwan pepper*
- *30ml/2tbsp vegetable oil*

DIPPING SAUCE:

- *150ml/5fl oz rice or white wine vinegar*
- *45ml/3 tbsp clear honey*
- *1 red chilli, sliced*
- *1 tbsp toasted sesame seeds*

METHOD:

Combine the fish cake ingredients and season with salt and pepper. Shape into 10 small patties. Bring the vinegar and honey to the boil in a small pan and boil for 5 minutes until reduced by half. Stir in the chilli and sesame seeds. Heat the oil in a large frying pan and cook the fish cakes for 3 minutes on each side.

Serve as a starter with the dipping sauce or with rice and stir-fried vegetables as a more substantial meal, pouring over the dipping sauce.

FISH STEW

This classic Italian dish makes a hearty meal, with fresh bread to mop up the juices, or served over potatoes or rice. Saffron adds colour and flavour, but can be omitted.

SERVES 2

30 minutes

★★

INGREDIENTS:

- pinch of saffron, soaked in boiling water
- 30ml/2 tbsp olive oil
- 2 garlic cloves, crushed
- 1 red or green chilli, de-seeded and chopped
- 1 onion, halved and sliced
- 400g/14oz tin peeled chopped tomatoes
- 100ml/3½fl oz white wine
- 2 bay leaves
- 3 sprigs fresh thyme or 1 tsp dried thyme
- 400g/14oz firm white fish (e.g. cod, monkfish), skinned and cut into chunks
- 12 mussels, cleaned and de-bearded
- 12 prawns or small squid
- salt and pepper

METHOD:

To clean mussels, rinse or scrub them in cold water and remove the protruding clump of hair (the 'beard') by pulling downwards with a sharp tug. This is known as 'de-bearding'.

Heat the oil in a large pan, add the garlic, chilli and onion and cook gently for 5 minutes. Add the tomatoes, wine and 200ml/7fl oz of water and bring to the boil. Add the bay leaves and thyme and simmer for 10 minutes. Season with salt and pepper, and add the saffron and all the fish. Cover and cook for 5 minutes. Take out the thyme sprigs and any unopened mussels – it is recommended that unopened mussels be thrown out as they may be contaminated. Serve.

REAL MEN DO EAT QUICHE!

FISHERMAN'S PIE

SERVES 2
1 hour 20 minutes
★★

INGREDIENTS:

- 150g/5oz firm white fish fillets, skinned
- 150g/5oz smoked haddock, skinned
- 110g/4oz peas
- 110g/4oz corn kernels
- 110g/4oz carrots, sliced
- 30ml/2 tbsp oil or butter
- 2 tbsp plain flour
- 250ml/9fl oz fish stock
- 2 medium potatoes, chopped
- 50ml/1½fl oz skimmed milk
- 30g/1oz cheese, grated (optional)
- salt and pepper

METHOD:

Heat the oven to 180°C/350°F/Gas Mark 4. Boil the potatoes for 20 minutes until tender, drain and mash with the milk. Cut the fish into large chunks and place in an ovenproof dish. Sprinkle with the vegetables. Heat the oil or butter in a small saucepan and mix in the flour. Cook for 2 minutes, but do not let it brown. Mix in the stock and cook for 2 more minutes until thick, season with salt and pepper. Pour this over the fish and vegetables. Spread with the mashed potato, scatter with the cheese if using and bake for 30–40 minutes until golden.

TUNA & CANNELLINI BEAN SALAD

SERVES 2
5 minutes
★

INGREDIENTS:

- 1 red onion, finely sliced
- 1 garlic clove, crushed
- 30ml/2 tbsp of olive oil
- juice of 1 lemon
- 15g/½oz fresh parsley, chopped
- 400g/14oz cooked cannellini beans, drained
- 225g/7½oz tinned tuna in brine, drained
- salt and pepper to taste
- 12 black olives (optional)

METHOD:

Gently combine all the ingredients, taking care not to crush the beans or flake the tuna too much. Serve with crusty bread or the potato focaccia from page 36.

LEMON & BASIL SALMON WITH PESTO MASH

SERVES 2

1 hour

★

INGREDIENTS:

- 2 x 150–200g/5–6½oz pieces of salmon fillet
- 1 lemon, juice and zest
- 15g/½oz basil
- 330g/11oz potatoes
- 100ml/3½fl oz skimmed milk
- 1–2 tbsp pesto
- salt and pepper

METHOD:

Preheat the oven to 200°C/400°F/Gas Mark 6. Bring the potatoes to the boil with salted water to cover, then reduce to simmer and cook, part covered, for 25 minutes, or until tender. While they are boiling, slit the salmon pieces in half and stuff with the basil leaves. Place in tin foil and sprinkle on the lemon juice and zest, salt and pepper and seal the foil. Bake for 15–20 minutes (15 minutes if your fish is very fresh and you like it rare, and 20 if you like it well done). When the potatoes are cooked, drain and place back in the saucepan and cover with a tea towel (this dries out the potatoes). Heat the milk and then mash into the potatoes. Beat in the pesto, and salt and pepper to taste. Pile onto plates, and top with the salmon.

LEMON-CRUSTED COD WITH FIVE-MINUTE RATATOUILLE

SERVES 2
45 minutes
★★

INGREDIENTS:

◆ *2 x 150–200g/5–6½oz pieces of cod fillet*
◆ *4 slices wholemeal bread, crumbled*
◆ *30ml/2 tbsp olive oil*
◆ *juice and zest of 1 lemon*
◆ *2 tbsp parsley, finely chopped*
◆ *50g/1½oz flaked almonds*
◆ *1 small onion, finely chopped*
◆ *1 courgette, finely chopped*
◆ *1 red pepper, finely shredded*
◆ *1 yellow pepper, finely shredded*
◆ *2 tomatoes, skinned, de-seeded and chopped*
◆ *salt and pepper*

METHOD:

Preheat the oven to 200°C/400°F/Gas Mark 6. Combine the breadcrumbs, 15ml/1 tbsp of oil, lemon zest, parsley and almonds. Place the cod in an ovenproof dish and top with the crumbs. Sprinkle with the lemon juice and season with salt and pepper. Bake for 20–30 minutes. In a medium-sized frying pan, heat the remaining oil and cook the onion for about 5 minutes until tender, then add the remaining ingredients and stir-fry for 5 more minutes. Serve the cod and ratatouille with some new potatoes.

MOROCCAN FISH SOUP

SERVES 2

15 minutes

★

INGREDIENTS:

- 15ml / 1 tbsp olive oil
- 1 large onion, sliced
- 2 garlic cloves, crushed
- 15g/½oz fresh parsley, chopped
- 2 tsp ground cumin
- 750ml / 1¼ pints fish stock
- 1 tsp salt (optional)
- 2 tsp harissa paste or chilli powder
- 200g / 6½oz cooked chickpeas
- 330g / 11oz firm white fish fillets, skinned
- 10g / ⅓ oz coriander, chopped

METHOD:

Heat the oil in a large pan and fry the onions, garlic, parsley and cumin for 3 minutes. Add the stock and season with the salt if needed and the harissa or chilli. Bring to the boil and add the chickpeas then the fish. Reduce the temperature and cook for 10 minutes until the fish is cooked through. Stir through the coriander. Spoon some rice or couscous into 2 bowls and pour over the hot soup.

REAL MEN DO EAT QUICHE!

MUSSELS WITH BLACK BEAN SAUCE

Mussels are cheap and high in iron, and not as much hassle to prepare as they might seem.

SERVES 2

15 minutes

★★★

INGREDIENTS:

- 250ml/8fl oz white wine
- 2 garlic cloves, sliced
- 15g/½oz fresh parsley, chopped
- 1kg/2lbs 2oz fresh mussels, scrubbed and de-bearded (see page 11)
- 250g/8oz egg noodles or spaghetti
- 45ml/3 tbsp black bean sauce
- 1 tsp cornflour, mixed with 15ml/1tbsp water•
- 15ml/1tbsp soy sauce

METHOD:

Bring the wine to the boil in a large pot with about 1cm/½ inch of water. Add the garlic, the mussels and half of the parsley, and cover. Steam for 4–5 minutes – the shells should be open. Remove the open mussels and cover for about 1 more minute. Remove all the mussels, discarding the unopened ones. Remove the flesh from the inside of the mussels, set aside. Cook the noodles or pasta according to the packet instructions. Strain the mussel/wine juice into a smaller pan and bring to the boil. Stir in the black bean sauce, soy sauce and cornflour and cook for about 1 minute until thickened. Stir in the shell-less mussels and serve over the drained noodles or pasta, garnish with the remaining parsley.

•Cornflour needs to be mixed or 'slackened' with a small amount of water before it is combined with other ingredients to prevent it forming lumps.

QUICK FISH CURRY

This is a great way to prepare fish for people who are not big fish fans, and of course for fish lovers. The curry and the creamy coconut taste go wonderfully with almost any white or red skinned fish.

SERVES 2

30 minutes

★

INGREDIENTS:

- 15ml/1tbsp groundnut oil
- 1 onion, sliced
- 2 garlic cloves, crushed
- 1 tbsp curry powder
- 1 tsp turmeric
- ½ tsp ground cumin
- 400g/14oz fish fillet (e.g. cod, gurnard, snapper)
- 150ml/5fl oz of coconut milk
- 1 large carrot, grated
- 1 tsp mustard seeds (optional)
- 15g/½oz coriander, chopped (optional)
- lemon or lime wedges to serve

METHOD:

Heat a medium frying pan and add the oil, onions, garlic, curry powder, turmeric and cumin and sauté until golden – about 5 minutes. Add the fish fillets and cook for 5 minutes. Turn over and add the coconut milk, 150ml/5fl oz water and the carrot and cook for a further 5–10 minutes, depending on the thickness of the fish. If using, dry fry the mustard seeds in a small pan until they pop, about 2 minutes. Serve the fish with rice and scatter over the coriander and mustard seeds. Serve with rice and pitta bread, and garnish with lemon or lime wedges.

SALADE NIÇOISE STUFFED LOAF

This is a great food for a picnic, or served at home for lunch or a light supper.

SERVES 2

10 minutes

★★★

INGREDIENTS:

- ◆ *1 x 400g/14oz wholemeal loaf*
- ◆ *1 garlic clove, crushed*
- ◆ *2 tomatoes, de-seeded and chopped*
- ◆ *¼ cucumber, de-seeded and chopped*
- ◆ *1 medium potato, cooked and sliced*
- ◆ *150g/5oz string beans, cooked*
- ◆ *10 black olives, pitted*
- ◆ *2 anchovy fillets, chopped*
- ◆ *2 tbsp capers*
- ◆ *15ml/1 tbsp olive oil*
- ◆ *15ml/1 tbsp balsamic or red wine vinegar*
- ◆ *salt and pepper*
- ◆ *flat-leaved parsley (optional)*

METHOD:

Cut the lid off the loaf and reserve and scrape out the bread inside, leaving a rim of 2cm/1 inch. Crumble the bread you have removed and reserve. Combine all the ingredients in a large bowl and add about 55g/2oz of the reserved crumbs. Fill the hollow loaf with the salad and replace the top. Wrap well in tinfoil and place in the fridge with something heavy on top to weight it down. Chill overnight. Unwrap and slice into 4. Serve garnished with flat-leaved parsley, if using.

SEAFOOD GUMBO

Creole gumbo is traditionally thickened with file powder, but it is hard to find unless you live in America, so it is not included in this version.

SERVES 2

30 minutes

★★

INGREDIENTS:

◆ *15ml/1 tbsp rapeseed oil*

◆ *1 onion, sliced*

◆ *2 garlic cloves, crushed*

◆ *1 carrot, sliced*

◆ *2 celery stalks, sliced*

◆ *1 green pepper, sliced*

◆ *750ml/1¼ pints fish or chicken stock*

◆ *100g/3½oz long-grain wild rice*

◆ *1 tsp salt (optional)*

◆ *400g/14oz mixed seafood (e.g. mussels, prawns, squid rings, cod) cut into bite-sized pieces*

◆ *100g/3½oz okra, trimmed (optional)*

◆ *Tabasco sauce*

◆ *lemon wedges to serve*

METHOD:

Heat the oil in a large pot and gently cook the onion, garlic, carrot, celery and pepper for 5 minutes. Add the stock and bring to the boil then add the rice and the salt if needed. Simmer for 15 minutes. Stir in the seafood and okra, if using, and cook for a further 5 minutes. Season with Tabasco to taste and serve with lemon wedges and crusty bread.

SMOKED HADDOCK CRÊPES

SERVES 2

30 minutes

★★

INGREDIENTS:

- 100g/3½oz wholemeal flour, sifted
- 55g/2oz plain flour, sifted
- 1 tsp salt
- 250ml/9fl oz skimmed milk
- 2 eggs, beaten
- 1 medium potato, grated
- 330g/11oz smoked haddock, skinned, cooked and flaked
- 200g/6½oz non-fat fromage frais
- 15g/½oz fresh parsley, chopped
- 15ml/1tbsp oil

METHOD:

Combine the flours and salt in a bowl. Gradually add the milk and then the eggs, and blend well. Stir in the potato and let sit for 10 minutes. Preheat the oven to 180°C/ 350°F/Gas Mark 4. Combine the haddock, fromage frais and parsley. Heat about ¼ of the oil in a non-stick pan, and pour in ¼ of the pancake mixture. Cook over a low–medium heat for 1–2 minutes until set and brown. Flip over and cook another 3 minutes. Repeat until 4 are made. Fill with the smoked haddock mixture and roll up. Place in a small ovenproof dish and cover. Bake for 15 minutes until the filling is piping hot.

SMOKED MACKEREL HASH

SERVES 2

30 minutes

★

INGREDIENTS:

- ◆ *15ml/1 tbsp rapeseed oil*
- ◆ *1 leek, chopped*
- ◆ *6 spring onions, chopped*
- ◆ *4 medium potatoes, boiled and cubed*
- ◆ *2 fillets smoked mackerel, skinned and flaked*
- ◆ *150ml/5fl oz skimmed milk*
- ◆ *85g/3oz watercress, chopped*
- ◆ *fresh chives and sour cream to serve (optional)*

METHOD:

Heat half the oil in a large frying pan and cook the leek for 10 minutes over a low heat. Set aside. Heat the remaining oil and add the spring onions, potatoes and mackerel and cook, constantly scraping the bottom and adding the milk slowly, for 15 minutes until the milk is used up and the mixture is golden. Stir in the watercress and leeks and heat about 3 minutes more. Serve scattered with chives and a dollop of sour cream.

SMOKED MACKEREL KEDGEREE

Kedgeree is a traditional breakfast dish, but is substantial enough to serve as lunch or supper. Mackerel, although an oily fish, is very high in essential fatty acids and omega 3, which help maintain a healthy heart.

SERVES 2
15 minutes
★

INGREDIENTS:

- 15ml/1 tbsp rapeseed oil
- 1 red onion, finely sliced
- 1 garlic clove, crushed
- ½ tsp turmeric
- 1 tsp curry powder
- 250g/8oz cooked and cooled basmati rice
- 250g/8oz smoked mackerel, skinned and flaked
- salt and pepper
- 10g/⅓oz fresh parsley, chopped
- 1 egg

METHOD:

Boil the egg for 6–8 minutes. Run under cold water, peel and quarter. Heat the oil in a frying pan and add the onion, garlic, turmeric and curry powder and cook for 2 minutes. Stir in the cooked rice, fish and 30ml/2 tbsp water. Cover and allow to heat through for about 2 minutes. Season to taste and stir in the parsley and egg quarters. Serve with hot toast or a green salad and lemon wedges.

SOLE WITH TOMATO & CINNAMON

This unusual Middle Eastern combination works extremely well. Serve it with steamed vegetables and flat breads.

SERVES 2

40 minutes

★

INGREDIENTS:

- 15ml/1 tbsp olive oil
- 1 onion, sliced
- 2 tsp ground cinnamon
- 2 large potatoes, sliced
- 400g/14oz tin of tomato soup
- 250ml/9fl oz fish or vegetable stock
- 2 sole fillets
- 15g/½oz parsley or coriander, chopped

METHOD:

Heat the oil in a large, heavy-based pan, or casserole, and cook the onion for 5 minutes. Add the cinnamon, potatoes, tomato soup and stock. Cover and simmer for 20 minutes or until the potatoes are tender. Place the sole fillets on top and sprinkle with the parsley or coriander. Cover and cook for 5 minutes then serve.

SQUID SALAD WITH LIME DRESSING

Either buy squid already cleaned, or ask your fishmonger to do it for you. As an alternative to squid, you could substitute 300–400g/10–14oz of sliced chicken breast and stir-fry for an extra 4 minutes.

SERVES 2
15 minutes
★★

INGREDIENTS:
- ◆ *400g/14oz cleaned squid bodies and tentacles (optional)*
- ◆ *30ml/2 tbsp groundnut oil*
- ◆ *3cm/1½inch fresh ginger, grated*
- ◆ *1–2 mild red chillies, de-seeded and finely chopped*
- ◆ *1 garlic clove, crushed*
- ◆ *2 sticks of lemon grass, peeled and finely sliced*
- ◆ *30ml/2 tbsp Thai fish sauce*
- ◆ *15ml/1 tbsp lime juice*
- ◆ *150g/5oz mixed salad leaves*
- ◆ *1 small avocado, chopped*
- ◆ *15g/½oz fresh coriander, chopped*

METHOD:
If the squid is small, slice down one side, to open out and criss-cross slash one side. If the squid is large, slice into 2cm/1inch wide rings, set aside with tentacles, if using. Heat a large frying pan to very hot and add 15ml/1 tbsp of the oil, the squid and the next 4 ingredients, quickly stir-fry until squid is cooked – about 2 minutes. Take off the heat, remove the squid and add the fish sauce, lime juice and remaining oil to the pan – it will warm through with the heat of the pan. Divide the salad and avocado between 2 plates, top with squid and drizzle with dressing. Scatter with fresh coriander.

SWEET & SOUR FISH

This sweet and sour dish goes well with rice. It is not always essential to stir-fry food in oil. If it is not important for the flavour, food can be 'steam fried' in water, which will start the cooking process the same way.

SERVES 2

15 minutes

★★

INGREDIENTS:

- ◆ 4 spring onions, shredded
- ◆ 3cm/1½ inch fresh ginger, shredded
- ◆ 1 red chilli, sliced (optional)
- ◆ 2 medium carrots, julienned
- ◆ 1 red and green pepper, julienned (cut into thin batons)
- ◆ 250g/8oz tin of pineapple chunks
- ◆ 2 tsp cornflour, slackened with 15ml/1 tbsp water
- ◆ 15ml/1 tbsp white wine vinegar
- ◆ 1 tsp sugar (optional)
- ◆ 2 x 150–200g/5–6½oz fillets of fish
- ◆ salt

METHOD:

Heat 100ml/3½fl oz water in a medium pan. Place the onions, ginger, carrots, chilli and pepper in the pan and steam fry for 2 minutes. Add the pineapple with juice, cornflour and vinegar and cook until thickened. Add the sugar if needed and a little salt. Grill or pan-fry the fish for about 5 minutes on each side and then pour over the sweet and sour sauce.

This chapter covers a variety of healthy, delicious recipes based on carbohydrates, such as bread, noodles and, of course, pasta – energy-rich foods that are guaranteed to stir even the laziest couch potato!

Pasta is very easy to cook, and makes a great base for almost any sauce. It will be the topping you choose that makes the dish healthy or not, so this chapter is full of ideas to make nutritious, filling pasta dishes. You can substitute wholewheat pasta, which is higher in dietary fibre, in any of the recipes. When cooking pasta, always boil in plenty of water and do not overcook it, it should be al dente, which means 'to the tooth', firm not soft.

CANNELLONI WITH BEANS & HERBS

Butter beans make a great creamy filling for cannelloni.

SERVES 2

50 minutes

★★

INGREDIENTS:

- 200g/6½oz butter beans, soaked overnight
- 1 leek, chopped
- 2 garlic cloves, crushed
- 15g/½oz fresh rosemary
- 15g/½oz fresh thyme
- 1 large potato, cooked and mashed
- 150g/5oz cannelloni shells
- 400g/14oz tin tomatoes, chopped
- salt and pepper
- Parmesan to serve

METHOD:

Drain the beans and place in a medium saucepan with plenty of water, bring to the boil and boil rapidly for 10 minutes. Skim any foam off the surface and add the leek, garlic, rosemary and thyme and lower the heat to a simmer. Simmer for about 1 hour until the beans are tender making sure they don't boil dry. Preheat the oven to 180°C/350°F/Gas Mark 4. Drain the beans and remove the rosemary and thyme stalks. Mix with the potato and season with salt and pepper. Spoon the filling into the cannelloni tubes and lay side by side in an ovenproof dish. Pour over the chopped tomatoes, season, and bake for 30 minutes. Serve with a light green salad, and shaved parmesan.

ARTICHOKE, WALNUT & MUSHROOM PIZZA

Everybody loves pizza, but it can be oily and excessively covered in cheese. Try topping pizza dough with less cheese and more nutritious vegetables such as the ones in this recipe. If time is short, use ready-made pizza base mix.

SERVES 2–4
1 hour 30 minutes
★★

INGREDIENTS:
- 250g/8oz strong bread flour
- 100g/3½oz wholemeal flour
- 1 sachet easy-blend yeast
- 1 tsp salt
- 250ml/9fl oz warm water
- 250g/8oz mushrooms, sliced
- 400g/14oz tin artichoke hearts, drained and quartered
- 50g/1½oz walnut pieces
- 15ml/1 tbsp olive oil
- 1 garlic clove, finely chopped
- 2 tbsp fresh chopped herbs (e.g. parsley, basil, oregano)
- salt and pepper

METHOD:
Combine the flours, yeast and salt in a large bowl and mix in the water to form a dough. Knead on a surface sprinkled with flour for about 5 minutes. Lightly oil the bowl and put the dough back in, cover with cling film and let rise in a warm place for about 45 minutes. Preheat the oven to 200°C/400°F/Gas Mark 6. Punch down the dough and roll and stretch out to a 30cm/12 inch diameter circle. Scatter the mushrooms, artichokes and walnuts. Sprinkle with oil, garlic and herbs and salt and pepper to taste. Bake for 20–25 minutes.

FRESH
TOMATO SAUCE

Fresh home-made tomato sauce makes a wonderful sauce for plain pasta or ravioli. It is also a tasty, easy way to add flavour to any grilled fish or chicken.

SERVES 2

10 minutes

★★

INGREDIENTS:

- ◆ *15ml/1 tbsp olive oil*
- ◆ *2 garlic cloves, crushed*
- ◆ *15g/½oz parsley, finely chopped*
- ◆ *6 large tomatoes, peeled, de-seeded and chopped*
- ◆ *15g/½oz fresh basil torn into small pieces*

OPTIONAL EXTRAS:

- ◆ *10 black or green olives, pitted*
- ◆ *4 anchovy fillets, chopped*
- ◆ *30g/1oz capers*

METHOD:

Heat the oil in a medium-sized pan and add the garlic and parsley and cook for 2 minutes. Stir in the tomatoes and cook for about 5 minutes until the tomatoes start to break up. If using any extra flavourings add them now and heat through for about 2 minutes. Take off the heat and stir in the basil.

FARFALLE WITH SMOKED CHICKEN

Whole chicken breasts can often be bought smoked at large supermarkets and butchers. If none are available, use ordinary cooked chicken breast, or the equivalent amount of sliced chicken.

SERVES 2

30 minutes

★

INGREDIENTS:

- ◆ *30ml/2 tbsp olive oil*
- ◆ *2 garlic cloves, crushed*
- ◆ *15g/½oz fresh parsley, chopped*
- ◆ *2 lemons – juice of both, zest of one*
- ◆ *2 smoked or cooked chicken breasts, sliced or 250g/8oz sliced smoked chicken*
- ◆ *250g/8oz farfalle (bows) pasta*
- ◆ *250g/8oz spinach, washed, chopped*
- ◆ *salt and pepper*
- ◆ *Parmesan cheese to serve (optional)*

METHOD:

Bring a large pan of salted water to the boil and cook the farfalle for about 12 minutes. Meanwhile heat the oil in a medium frying pan and cook the garlic and parsley for 3 minutes. Add the chicken and lemon juice, zest, salt and pepper, cover and cook for 5 minutes. Lightly steam the spinach: place it in a large pan with 50ml/2fl oz of water, cover and steam for 2 minutes. Drain the farfalle and mix in a large pot with the chicken. Serve on a bed of spinach, with Parmesan cheese if using.

PARSNIP & CARROT FRITTATA

Frittata or its Spanish equivalent, tortilla, are more substantial versions of an omelette. Carrot and parsnips add a nice twist, making it a perfect winter meal, or in summer, try different vegetables such as peppers or courgettes.

SERVES 4

50 minutes

★★★

INGREDIENTS:

◆ *30ml/2 tbsp olive oil*
◆ *2 medium-large potatoes, sliced*
◆ *1 mild onion, sliced*
◆ *1 garlic clove, crushed*
◆ *1 carrot, sliced*
◆ *1 parsnip, sliced*
◆ *3 eggs*
◆ *1 tsp salt*
◆ *ground pepper*

METHOD:

Heat 15ml/1 tbsp of the oil in a medium frying pan and gently cook the potatoes, onion, garlic, carrot and parsnip for 20 minutes over a low heat, covering it for the first 10 minutes. Lightly beat the eggs, salt and pepper in a large bowl, then add the potato mixture and stir well. Heat the remaining oil in the pan and tip in the potato and egg mixture. Press down, firmly and evenly and cook over a medium heat for 10 minutes. Slide the frittata out onto a plate. Hold the pan over it and flip it back in. Cook for a further 10 minutes. Serve either hot or chilled sliced into wedges.

MEXICAN-STYLE PASTA

Pasta and beans is a common combination in Italy, but why not try it with this Mexican salsa-style sauce. You could add cooked prawns or chicken for a change.

SERVES 2

15 minutes

★

INGREDIENTS:

- 1 red onion, chopped
- 2 garlic cloves, crushed
- 6 large tomatoes, peeled, de-seeded and chopped
- 1 tbsp tomato purée
- 400g/14oz tin black-eyed beans, drained
- 15g/½oz fresh coriander, chopped
- 1–2 tsp Tabasco sauce or chilli powder
- salt and pepper
- 330g/11oz fusilli pasta (spirals) or radiatore
- 1 avocado, cubed (optional)

METHOD:

Boil the pasta, according to the packet instructions. In a medium pan, combine the onion, garlic, tomatoes, purée and black-eyed beans. Cook for about 5 minutes until the beans are hot through. Season with the Tabasco sauce or chilli powder and some salt.

Lastly, stir in the coriander and serve the sauce over the pasta with the avocado on top if using.

PENNE WITH GREEN BEANS & WALNUT SAUCE

SERVES 2

20 minutes

★

INGREDIENTS:

- ◆ *100g/3½oz walnut pieces, finely chopped*
- ◆ *15ml/1 tbsp olive oil*
- ◆ *4 shallots, finely chopped*
- ◆ *2 garlic cloves, crushed*
- ◆ *180g/6oz low-fat crème fraîche*
- ◆ *250g/8oz green beans, cut into 6cm/2½ inch pieces, blanched*
- ◆ *250g/8oz penne pasta*
- ◆ *salt and pepper*
- ◆ *Parmesan cheese (optional)*

METHOD:

Bring a large pan of salted water to the boil and cook the penne for 12 minutes. While it is cooking, heat the oil in a medium-sized pan and gently cook the shallots, garlic and walnuts for 5 minutes. Stir in the crème fraîche and heat through. Add the blanched beans and season with salt and pepper. Drain the penne and combine with the sauce. Serve with Parmesan cheese, if using.

PASTA RIBBONS WITH COTTAGE CHEESE & GREENS

SERVES 2
15 minutes
★

INGREDIENTS:

- *250g/8oz pappardelle or other flattish pasta (e.g. tagliatelle or farfalle)*
- *15ml/1 tbsp olive oil*
- *2 garlic cloves, crushed*
- *1 onion, finely chopped*
- *15g/½oz flat leaf parsley, chopped*
- *75g/2½oz rocket or watercress, chopped*
- *250g/8oz low-fat cottage cheese*
- *50g/1½oz Parmesan cheese, grated, some shavings reserved for garnish*

METHOD:

Bring a large pot of salted water to the boil and cook the pasta according to packet instructions. Meanwhile, heat the olive oil in a medium saucepan and cook the garlic, onion and parsley over a gentle heat until transparent and just turning golden, about 5 minutes. Stir in the rocket or watercress and toss to wilt. Take off the heat and stir in the cheeses. Drain the pasta and quickly stir through the cheese mixture. Serve garnished with Parmesan and a few rocket or watercress sprigs.

PUMPKIN GNOCCHI WITH SPINACH

Gnocchi is very like pasta but the addition of potatoes makes it more dumpling-like.

SERVES 2

40 minutes

★★★

INGREDIENTS:

- ◆ *200g/6½oz potatoes, peeled and cubed*
- ◆ *200g/6½oz pumpkin, peeled and cubed*
- ◆ *1 egg, beaten*
- ◆ *150g/5½oz plain flour, plus extra for dusting*
- ◆ *100g/3½oz spinach, washed and chopped*
- ◆ *50g/1½oz Parmesan cheese, grated*
- ◆ *salt and pepper*
- ◆ *nutmeg to taste*

METHOD:

Boil the potatoes and pumpkin until tender, drain and cover with a tea towel for 5 minutes to dry out. Mash very well until smooth, season, then beat in the egg and flour (if you are using very watery pumpkin, you may need more flour). The mixture should be a fairly soft dough. Heat the oven to 180°C/350°F/Gas Mark 4 and lightly oil a small casserole dish. Line the bottom with the spinach. Sprinkle a work surface with flour and roll out the dough to 1.5cm/½ inch thickness. Cut out 5cm/2 inch circles and place these overlapping on the spinach. Sprinkle with nutmeg and cheese and bake for 30 minutes. Serve piping hot with a fresh spinach salad.

35

POTATO & ROSEMARY FOCACCIA

Potato focaccia makes a great meal: it is comfort food at its finest, bread and potato all in one. After it is baked, try topping it with some fresh baby spinach or rocket and shavings of Parmesan cheese.

SERVES 2

1 hour

★★★

INGREDIENTS:

- 150g/5oz mashed potato
- 250g/8oz strong white bread flour, sifted
- 1 sachet easy blend yeast
- 1 tsp salt
- 30ml/2 tbsp olive oil
- 200ml/7fl oz warm water
- 1 medium-large potato, scrubbed and sliced thinly
- 4 tsp fresh rosemary, off the stalk, or 2 tsp dried
- salt and pepper

METHOD:

In a large bowl, combine the potatoes, flour, yeast, salt and 15ml/1 tbsp of olive oil and mix in enough water to form a soft dough (you may not need all the water). Knead lightly and cover with cling film and leave to rise for about 1 hour. Preheat the oven to 180°C/350°F/Gas Mark 4. Lightly oil a large baking tray. Place the dough in the middle and work out to the edges to form a square or rectangle. Top the dough with the potato slices and the rosemary season, and drizzle with the remaining oil. Bake for 50 minutes, covering if the focaccia is getting too brown.

SPAGHETTI BAKE

This is a good way to use up left-over spaghetti, or any other pasta for that matter. The combination of vegetables used can be altered according to what you have in the fridge.

SERVES 2

40 minutes

★

INGREDIENTS:

- ◆ 15ml/1 tbsp olive oil
- ◆ 2 garlic cloves, crushed
- ◆ 1 onion, chopped
- ◆ 400g/14oz tin tomatoes, chopped
- ◆ 250g/8oz cooked spaghetti
- ◆ 1 large carrot, sliced
- ◆ 1 courgette, sliced
- ◆ 100g/3½oz cauliflower, in small florets
- ◆ 100g/3½oz broccoli, in small florets
- ◆ 50g/1½oz sunflower seeds
- ◆ 2 tsp mixed herbs
- ◆ 50g/1½oz goat's cheese, or low-fat cheddar grated
- ◆ salt and pepper

METHOD:

Preheat the oven to 180°C/350°F/Gas Mark 4. Heat the oil in a medium pan and sauté the onion and garlic for a few minutes then add the tomatoes and boil for about 5 minutes. Combine this sauce with all the remaining ingredients except the cheese. Mix well and season with salt and pepper. Pile into a roasting dish or casserole and pat down. Sprinkle with the cheese and bake for 30 minutes.

PUMPKIN, SWEET POTATO & ORANGE PASTA

SERVES 2

30 minutes

★

INGREDIENTS:

- *15ml/1 tbsp olive oil*
- *2 garlic cloves, crushed*
- *6 shallots, chopped*
- *1 butternut squash, peeled and chopped into 2cm/1inch dice*
- *1 large sweet potato, peeled and chopped into 2cm/1 inch dice*
- *2 oranges, juice of both, zest of one*
- *330ml/11fl oz chicken or vegetable stock*
- *3 tbsp fresh parsley, chopped*
- *250g/8oz pasta shapes*
- *salt and pepper*

METHOD:

Bring a large pot of salted water to the boil. Heat the oil in a large saucepan and gently fry the garlic and shallots for 5 minutes. Add the squash, sweet potato, orange juice, zest and stock. Bring to the boil and then reduce the heat and simmer un-covered, for about 15 minutes, until the vegetables are soft but not mushy. Meanwhile, cook the pasta according to the packet instructions. When the vegetables are done, remove and keep warm. Bring the remaining liquid to the boil and reduce to about 50ml/2fl oz. Season with salt and pepper. Toss this, with the vegetables, parsley and the drained pasta.

TOMATO & TUNA PASTA

SERVES 2
25 minutes
★

INGREDIENTS:

- ◆ *15ml/1 tbsp olive oil*
- ◆ *2 garlic cloves, crushed*
- ◆ *1 onion, finely chopped*
- ◆ *15g/½oz fresh parsley, chopped*
- ◆ *100ml/3½fl oz white or red wine, optional*
- ◆ *400g/14oz tin chopped tomatoes*
- ◆ *200g/6½oz tin of tuna*
- ◆ *10 black or green olives (optional)*
- ◆ *340g/12oz pasta*
- ◆ *salt and pepper*
- ◆ *Parmesan cheese (optional)*

METHOD:

Bring a large pot of salted water to the boil. In a medium saucepan, heat the oil and gently fry the garlic, onion and the parsley (save about 1 tbsp to garnish) for 5 minutes. Add the wine if using and boil for 5 minutes until reduced by half. Add the tomatoes, salt and pepper and cook, stirring occasionally, for about 10 minutes. Cook the pasta in the boiling water, according to packet instructions. Just before the pasta is ready, add the tuna and olives, if using, to the tomato sauce and gently heat through. Drain the pasta and place in serving dishes topped with tomato and tuna sauce. Sprinkle with the reserved parsley and some extra ground pepper.

Serve with Parmesan cheese if using.

SPINACH & MUSHROOM LASAGNE

SERVES 4

1 hour 15 minutes

★★

INGREDIENTS:

- ◆ *1 medium onion, chopped*
- ◆ *2 garlic cloves, crushed*
- ◆ *30ml/2 tbsp olive oil*
- ◆ *15g/½oz fresh parsley, chopped*
- ◆ *250g/8oz mushrooms, sliced*
- ◆ *1 tsp salt*
- ◆ *400g/14oz tin chopped tomatoes*
- ◆ *1 tbsp flour*
- ◆ *100ml/3½fl oz skimmed milk*
- ◆ *250g/8oz low-fat cottage cheese*
- ◆ *100g/3½oz spinach, washed and chopped*
- ◆ *200g/6½oz lasagne sheets (cooked if needed as per packet instructions)*
- ◆ *50g/1½oz Parmesan cheese, grated*
- ◆ *salt and pepper*

METHOD:

Heat the oven to 180°C/350°F/Gas Mark 4. Heat 15ml/1 tbsp of oil in a medium saucepan and gently fry the garlic and parsley for 3 minutes. Add the mushrooms and salt and cook for 5 minutes. Add the tomatoes and cook for 10 minutes, stirring occasionally. Heat the remaining oil in a small saucepan, and gently cook the onion for 5 minutes over a low heat. Sprinkle on the flour and cook for 1 minute. Stir in the milk and turn the heat up to medium. Cook for 2 minutes until the sauce thickens. Take off the heat and cool slightly, then stir in the cottage cheese. Season lightly with salt and pepper. Lightly oil a small casserole dish and line the bottom with lasagne then spread with 1/4 of the cheese sauce then 1/3 spinach then 1/3 of the tomato sauce then more pasta. Repeat until all the ingredients are used, ending with a final layer of pasta and cheese sauce. Sprinkle with Parmesan cheese if using and bake for 40 minutes.

VEGETABLE STIR-FRY WITH PEANUT NOODLES

SERVES 2

15 minutes

★★

INGREDIENTS:

- 4 spring onions, diagonally sliced
- 2 garlic cloves, finely sliced
- 500g/1lb 2oz mixed vegetables of choice (e.g. peppers, carrots, broccoli, cabbage, beans, mangetout, mushrooms)
- 45ml/3 tbsp soy sauce
- 15ml/1 tbsp chilli sauce or ketchup
- 2 tsp cornflour, mixed with 15ml/1 tbsp of water·
- 250g/8oz egg or rice noodles
- 55g/1½oz peanuts, shelled and skinned
- 30ml/2 tbsp groundnut oil
- 15ml/1 tbsp white wine or rice vinegar
- 1 tsp sugar

METHOD:

In a blender, blend the peanuts, 15ml/1 tbsp of the oil, vinegar, sugar and 15ml/1 tbsp of the soy sauce with enough water to make a runny sauce. Set aside. Cook the noodles according to the packet instructions, drain and combine with the sauce. Heat the remaining oil and stir-fry the spring onions and garlic for 2 minutes. Add the vegetables and stir-fry for 5 minutes more. Combine the cornflour with the remaining soy and chilli sauce or ketchup. Stir this into the vegetables with a little water if necessary. Pile the vegetables on top of the noodles and serve.

·Cornflour needs to be mixed or 'slackened' with a small amount of water before it is combined with other ingredients to prevent it forming lumps.

41

VEGETABLE AND FETA CHEESE CALZONE

Calzone is almost like a pie or pastie, but without the pastry. It uses a bread dough to enclose its filling, which is steamed inside.

SERVES 2

1 hour 20 minutes

★★

INGREDIENTS:

- 250g/8oz strong bread flour, sifted, plus extra for dusting
- 100g/3½oz wholemeal flour
- 1 sachet easyblend yeast
- 1 tsp salt
- 1 red onion, sliced
- 1 red pepper, sliced
- 1 green pepper, sliced
- 1 garlic clove, crushed
- 2 tsp dried oregano
- 2 tbsp fresh oregano, chopped
- 150g/5½oz feta cheese, in 1cm/½ inch cubes

METHOD:

Combine the flours with the yeast and salt and mix in 250ml/9fl oz of warm water. Mix together then tip onto a floured work surface. Lightly oil the bowl then knead the dough for 5 minutes and return to the oiled bowl. Cover and leave to rise for about 40 minutes. Preheat the oven to 200°C/400°F/Gas Mark 6. Punch down the dough and roll and stretch out to 2 x 20cm/8 inch circles. Toss the remaining ingredients together and season with salt and pepper. Place half in the centre of each circle of dough. Brush the edges with water and fold over the dough to form a semi-circle. Press the edges together firmly and place on a floured baking sheet. Place in the oven and reduce the temperature to 180°C/350°F/Gas Mark 4. Bake for 30 minutes until golden.

WINTER VEGETABLE CALZONE

SERVES 2

1 hour 15 minutes

★★

INGREDIENTS:

- ◆ *250g/8oz strong bread flour, sifted, plus extra for dusting*
- ◆ *100g/3½oz wholemeal flour*
- ◆ *1 sachet easyblend yeast*
- ◆ *1 tsp salt*
- ◆ *15ml/1 tbsp olive oil*
- ◆ *1 medium carrot, chopped*
- ◆ *1 medium parsnip, cubed*
- ◆ *200g/6½oz swede, cubed*
- ◆ *1 medium leek, sliced*
- ◆ *1 medium potato, cubed*
- ◆ *1 tbsp horseradish*
- ◆ *salt and pepper*

METHOD:

Combine the flours with the yeast and salt and mix in 250ml/9fl oz of warm water. Mix together then tip onto a floured work surface. Lightly oil the bowl then knead the dough for 5 minutes and return to the oiled bowl. Cover and leave to rise for about 40 minutes. Preheat the oven to 200°C/400°F/Gas Mark 6. Punch down the dough and roll and stretch out to 2x 20cm/8 inch circles. Heat the oil in a large pan and cook the leeks gently for 5 minutes. Add the remaining vegetables and cover, cooking for 5 minutes more. Stir in the horseradish and some salt and pepper to taste. Place half into the centre of each circle of dough.

Brush the edges with water and fold the dough over to form a semi-circle. Press firmly together. Place on a floured baking sheet, place in the oven and reduce the temperature to 180°C/350°F/Gas Mark 4 and bake for 30 minutes, until golden.

REAL MEN DO EAT QUICHE!

Poultry is an excellent source of protein and, if skinned and trimmed, is low in fat. Keep the skin on when roasting a chicken, or it just won't be the same, but remember to remove it before eating! And turkey is not just for Christmas — it's a great, lean alternative to chicken, so try the recipes given or substitute it in one of the other dishes in this section.

When buying poultry (and eggs), always choose free-range when possible; you'll be supporting a worthwhile industry, and you'll find the meat tastes a lot better too.

BAKED CHICKEN WITH CARROT & ONION

This is a perfect alternative to roast chicken, which really needs the skin left on. It remains moist with its own juices and the skin is not necessary.

SERVES 4

2 hours

★★

INGREDIENTS:

- ◆ 1 small chicken (about 1.5kg/3lb 5oz)
- ◆ 1 lemon, peeled
- ◆ 15g/½oz fresh thyme, off the stalk, or 1 tbsp dried
- ◆ 4 medium carrots, sliced
- ◆ 2 large onions, sliced
- ◆ salt and pepper

METHOD:

Preheat the oven to 180°C/350°F/Gas Mark 4. Rinse the chicken and remove any giblets. Peel off the skin, cutting it away with a knife where necessary. Remove any excess fat (there is a lot around the back cavity). Sprinkle the centre with salt and pepper and stuff with the lemon and half of the thyme. Place the chicken in a casserole dish with a lid, or a roasting tin lined with enough tin foil to cover the chicken, leaving room for air to circulate. Surround the chicken with the carrots and onions and sprinkle with the remaining thyme, salt and pepper. Cover or seal the tin foil.

Bake for 1½ hours. Serve the chicken over rice or potato, with the onions and carrots in the chicken juices.

AVOCADO & CHICKEN CAESAR SALAD

Caesar salad is absolutely delicious, but traditionally high in fat. I have added avocado, this means the dressing remains creamy but is considerably lower in saturated fat. The addition of chicken makes it a very satisfying meal.

SERVES 2
15 minutes
★

INGREDIENTS:
- 1 small Cos lettuce, or 2 Little Gems, washed and torn into bite-sized pieces
- 2 chicken breasts, grilled and shredded
- 50g/1½oz Parmesan cheese, shaved or grated
- a small baguette, sliced

THE DRESSING:
- 1 avocado, mashed
- juice of 1 small lemon
- 1 garlic clove, crushed
- 5ml/1 tsp mustard
- a few drops Worcestershire sauce
- 2 anchovies, mashed (optional)
- salt and pepper

METHOD:
Heat the oven to 200°C/400°F/Gas Mark 6, place the baguette slices on a baking tray and bake for 5–10 minutes, until golden and crunchy. Combine the avocado, lemon, garlic, mustard, Worcestershire sauce and anchovies, if using, with enough water to make a runny dressing (about 100ml/3½fl oz). Season with salt and pepper. Arrange the lettuce and chicken on plates and drizzle over the dressing. Scatter with Parmesan and toast and serve.

CHICKEN CRUMBLE

SERVES 2

1 hour 30 minutes

★★

INGREDIENTS:

- 2 large pieces of chicken, on the bone (e.g. leg or thigh), skinned
- 2 cloves of garlic, crushed
- 2 onions, 1 peeled and chopped; 1 cut in half
- 15g/½oz parsley, chopped and stalks reserved
- ½ chicken stock cube
- 1 tbsp butter
- 1 tbsp flour
- 1 carrot, chopped
- 1 stick celery, chopped
- 1 small leek, chopped
- 3 slices wholemeal bread, crumbled
- 50g/1½oz nuts (e.g. almond, cashew, walnut), chopped

METHOD:

Place the chicken into a medium saucepan with 2 cups of water (or enough to cover), the whole onion, cut in half and add the parsley stalks. Bring to the boil and simmer uncovered for 20 minutes. Remove the chicken, cool and shred off the bone. Boil the remaining liquid to reduce to 150ml/5fl oz, then dissolve the stock cube in it. Strain if necessary and keep to one side. Heat the oven to 180°C/350°F/Gas Mark 4. Melt the butter in a small pan and gently fry the garlic and chopped onion for 5 minutes, then stir in the flour. Cook for 1 minute, then slowly add the reserved chicken stock stirring constantly to make a thick sauce.

Combine this sauce with the chicken, carrot, celery, leek and half the parsley. Spoon into a small casserole or ovenproof dish. Combine the breadcrumbs and remaining parsley and scatter over the chicken and sprinkle with the nuts. Bake for 30–40 minutes until piping hot.

CHICKEN BURRITOS

*This spicy chicken filling could be used to fill tacos or simply served over rice,
if soft flour tortillas are not available.*

SERVES 2
25 minutes
★

INGREDIENTS:

◆ *15ml/1 tbsp rapeseed oil*
◆ *2 garlic cloves, crushed*
◆ *1 onion, chopped*
◆ *1 tsp ground cumin*
◆ *1 tsp ground coriander*
◆ *½ tsp cayenne pepper*
◆ *2 chicken breasts,
skinned, cooked and
shredded*
◆ *1 red pepper, de-seeded
and sliced*
◆ *1 medium carrot,
chopped*
◆ *400g/14oz chopped
tomatoes*
◆ *15g/½oz fresh coriander*
◆ *4-6 soft flour tortillas*
◆ *a selection of lettuce,
tomatoes, avocado*
◆ *sour cream and re-fried
beans (see page 70)*

METHOD:

Heat the oil in a medium
pan and cook the garlic,
onion, cumin, coriander
and cayenne pepper for
5 minutes. Add the
pepper, carrot and
tomatoes and cook for
about 10 minutes. Stir in
the chicken and heat
through. Warm the
tortillas through. Stir the
coriander into the
chicken mixture and pile
onto the tortillas. Add
other toppings of choice.
Then roll up and serve.

CHICKEN WITH APRICOTS & ALMONDS

SERVES 2

1 hour

★

INGREDIENTS:

- 15ml/1 tbsp olive oil
- 1 large mild onion, sliced
- 7g/¼oz fresh thyme, off the stalk, or 2 tsp dried
- 2 leg or thigh pieces of chicken, skinned
- 1 tbsp flour
- 1 pkt onion soup mix
- 340g/12oz tin apricot halves
- 50g/1½oz almond flakes

METHOD:

Preheat the oven to 180°C/350°F/Gas Mark 4. Heat the oil in a large frying pan and brown the chicken for about 3 minutes on each side. Place the chicken into a roasting dish and sprinkle with the flour and then the onion soup mix. Scatter over the onions and thyme and then pour on the apricots with their syrup. Pour over water to almost cover the chicken. Cover and bake for 40 minutes then scatter on the almonds and bake for a further 10 minutes, uncovered. Serve with rice or couscous.

CHICKEN NOODLE SALAD

Use up left-over roast chicken or poach or grill a couple of breasts for this tasty summer meal.

SERVES 2

15 minutes

★

INGREDIENTS:

- 250g/8oz egg or rice noodles
- 4 spring onions, shredded
- 1 carrot, julienned
- 1 courgette, julienned
- 330g/11oz cooked chicken, shredded
- toasted sesame seeds (optional)
- 15g/½oz coriander, chopped

THE DRESSING:

- 1 garlic clove, crushed
- 15ml/1 tbsp rice or white wine vinegar
- 15ml/1 tbsp lemon juice
- 15ml/1 tbsp clear honey
- 15ml/1 tbsp chilli sauce
- 30ml/2 tbsp groundnut oil
- 5ml/1 tsp sesame seed oil (optional)

METHOD:

Combine the dressing ingredients. Cook the noodles according to packet instructions, drain and refresh in cold water. Drain well. Cut the carrot and courgette into matchsticks or ribbons using a vegetable peeler. Combine these with the spring onions, noodles, chicken, dressing and coriander and sprinkle with the sesame seeds if using.

CHILLI CHICKEN WITH WATER CHESTNUTS

Chinese styles of cooking are healthy as food is cooked quickly and with very little fat.

SERVES 2

15 minutes

★★

INGREDIENTS:

- ◆ *15ml/1 tbsp groundnut oil*
- ◆ *1 garlic clove, crushed*
- ◆ *4 spring onions, sliced diagonally*
- ◆ *2cm/1 inch fresh ginger, grated*
- ◆ *2 boneless chicken breasts, sliced*
- ◆ *15ml/1 tbsp chilli sauce*
- ◆ *30ml/2 tbsp light soy sauce*
- ◆ *15ml/1 tbsp clear honey*
- ◆ *220g/7½oz tin of water chestnuts, drained and sliced*

METHOD:

Heat the oil in a wok and stir fry the garlic, onions, ginger and chicken for 5–8 minutes, until the chicken is cooked through. Stir in the chilli, soy and honey, then the chestnuts and heat through. Serve with rice or noodles.

CHICKEN WITH ASPARAGUS

Asparagus goes wonderfully with chicken, and this recipe uses all the asparagus, not just the tender tips, so there is no waste.

SERVES 2
1 hour 15 minutes
★★

INGREDIENTS:

- *15ml / 1 tbsp olive oil*
- *2 medium potatoes, sliced*
- *1 leek sliced*
- *4 small chicken pieces (e.g. small breast, thigh, leg), skinned*
- *25g / 1oz butter*
- *2 tbsp flour*
- *salt and pepper*
- *250g / 8oz fresh asparagus*
- *200ml / 6½fl oz skimmed milk*
- *200ml / 6½fl oz chicken stock*
- *juice of 2 lemons*

METHOD:

Preheat the oven to 180°C/350°F/Gas Mark 4. Lightly oil a casserole dish and line the bottom with the potatoes. Place the chicken on top and sprinkle with the leek. Snap or cut the tough bottoms off the asparagus and chop into 1cm/½ inch pieces, reserving the tips. Scatter the asparagus ends over the chicken.

Melt the butter in a small pan, stir in the flour and cook for 2 minutes. Gradually stir in the milk and stock until it is all blended. Season with salt and pepper and pour over the chicken. Bake for 50 minutes. Add the asparagus tips, cover and bake for a further 10 minutes. Sprinkle with the lemon juice and serve.

GREEK CHICKEN & LEMON SOUP

This tangy soup makes full use of a chicken, but if you like, you could use chicken breasts and bought stock.

SERVES 4

1 hour and 15 minutes

★★

INGREDIENTS:

- ◆ *1 small chicken, skinned and trimmed*
- ◆ *1 onion, halved*
- ◆ *2 garlic cloves*
- ◆ *2 bay leaves*
- ◆ *7g/¼oz fresh oregano or thyme*
- ◆ *200g/6½oz long grain rice*
- ◆ *1 egg, beaten*
- ◆ *juice of 2 small lemons*
- ◆ *salt and pepper*

METHOD:

Place the chicken in a large pot with the onion, garlic, bay leaves and oregano or thyme and cover with water. Bring to simmering point and gently cook for about 1 hour. Cool in the pot and then remove the chicken and shred the flesh off the bones. Return the bones to the chicken water and bring to the boil. Continue boiling for about 30 minutes, then strain the stock. Bring back to the boil and add the rice. Cover and cook for 15 minutes. Season with salt and pepper. Quickly stir in the egg and lemon, then the shredded chicken and heat through.

REAL MEN DO EAT QUICHE!

EASY PEKING-STYLE CHICKEN

Peking duck is a delicious treat at Chinese restaurants but a long and fiddly job if you want to prepare it at home. This recipe is most untraditional but makes it easy to recreate Peking flavours. Chicken is less fatty than duck.

SERVES 2

2 hours 30 minutes

★

INGREDIENTS:
- 2 chicken breasts, skinned

THE MARINADE:
- 2 garlic cloves, crushed
- 1 tsp five spice powder
- 60ml/4 tbsp soy sauce
- 15ml/1 tbsp honey
- 10ml/2 tsp sesame oil
- 15ml/1 tbsp chilli sauce (optional)

TO SERVE:
- Chinese style pancakes or boiled rice
- half a cucumber, julienned
- 6 spring onions, shredded
- plum or hoisin sauce

METHOD:

Mix together the marinade ingredients in a large non-metal bowl or a plastic bag and cover the chicken. Marinade the chicken for at least 2 hours, preferably overnight. Preheat the oven to 180°C/350°F/ Gas Mark 4. Place the chicken in a small roasting dish and pour over the marinade. Cook for about 20 minutes. Cool for about 5 minutes and slice. Have the warmed pancakes or rice ready with the other garnishes. Guests can make up their own pancakes or you can serve the chicken slices over the rice.

ONE-POT CHICKEN WITH RICE

This all-in-one dish is so easy to prepare and with only one cooking pot, nobody can complain about doing the dishes.

SERVES 2

50 minutes

★

INGREDIENTS:

- ◆ *15ml/1 tbsp olive oil*
- ◆ *2 garlic cloves, crushed*
- ◆ *1 onion, sliced*
- ◆ *4 pieces chicken (e.g. breast, thigh), skinned*
- ◆ *1 tbsp mild paprika*
- ◆ *1 red, 1 green and 1 yellow pepper, sliced*
- ◆ *200g/6½oz par-boiled rice*
- ◆ *2 sticks celery, cut into 1cm/½ inch slices*
- ◆ *400g/14oz tin of chopped tomatoes*
- ◆ *chicken stock to cover, about 250ml/9fl oz*

METHOD:

Heat the oil in a large heavy-based saucepan or casserole and cook the onion and garlic for about 3 minutes until golden. Add the chicken and cook for 5 minutes until browned, then stir in the paprika and rice. Stir. Scatter with the peppers and celery and pour on the tomatoes and enough stock to cover the chicken. Bring to the boil. Cover tightly with a lid or foil and turn the heat down to very low. Simmer for 30 minutes until the chicken is cooked through and the rice is plump.

TANDOORI CHICKEN

SERVES 2
50 minutes
★

INGREDIENTS:

◆ *2 chicken legs or thigh pieces, skinned, rinsed and patted dry*
◆ *1 tsp salt*
◆ *250ml/9fl oz low-fat natural yoghurt*
◆ *juice of 1 lemon*
◆ *2 garlic cloves, crushed*
◆ *2 tbsp garam masala or tandoori paste*
◆ *3 tbsp fresh coriander to serve*

METHOD:
Slash the chicken pieces, diagonally at approx. 1cm/½ inch intervals. Rub with salt. Place in a non-metal bowl. In a separate bowl, mix all the remaining ingredients except the coriander and pour over the chicken. Cover and marinate in the fridge overnight, turning once or twice. Heat the oven or grill to very hot (220°C/425°F/Gas

Mark 7). Place the chicken in a roasting dish or under the grill and cook, turning once until the juices run clear, 40 minutes in the oven or 30 minutes if using the grill. Serve with boiled rice or naan bread and coriander.

TURKEY CHOW MEIN

SERVES 2
15 minutes
★

INGREDIENTS:

◆ *125g/4½oz egg noodles*
◆ *15ml/1 tbsp ground-nut oil*
◆ *2 garlic cloves, sliced*
◆ *2.5cm/1 inch piece root ginger, grated*
◆ *2 turkey breasts, skinned and sliced*
◆ *4 spring onions, diagonally sliced*
◆ *100g/3½oz bean sprouts*
◆ *1 red pepper, finely sliced*
◆ *15ml/1 tbsp chilli sauce*
◆ *15ml/1 tbsp soy sauce*

METHOD:
Bring a pan of water to the boil, then cook the noodles for 2 minutes. Rinse in cold water and drain well. Heat the oil in a wok or large frying pan. Add the garlic and ginger and cook for 1 minute. Add the turkey and cook for 3 minutes, then toss in the bean sprouts, spring

onions, red pepper and cook for 1 minute. Then toss in the sauces and noodles and fry for about 3 minutes. Serve.

NUT STUFFING FOR CHICKEN

This healthy stuffing can be used to stuff the Baked Chicken with Carrot and Onion on page 45.

STUFFS 1 SMALL CHICKEN

25 minutes

★

INGREDIENTS:

- 15ml / 1 tbsp olive oil
- 1 onion, finely chopped
- 2 garlic cloves, crushed
- 1 tbsp fresh parsley, chopped
- 100g / 3½oz nuts, chopped (e.g. almonds, walnuts)
- 100g / 3½oz wholemeal bread
- 1 lemon, or small orange, juice and zest
- 100ml / 3½ fl oz skimmed milk

METHOD:

Soak the bread in the milk for about 5 minutes then drain. Heat the oil in the frying pan and fry the onion and garlic for 3 minutes, then add the parsley and cook for another 2 minutes. Stir in the chopped nuts and cook for 5 minutes. Add the bread, the lemon juice and zest and mix to combine.

An easy alternative is to stuff the chicken with mashed potato mixed with spring onions and salt and pepper. It soaks up the chicken juices and is delicious.

QUICK COQ AU VIN

Coq au vin has always been a relatively simple dish to make, a great one-pot meal, but pieces of chicken with their skins on make it quite oily. Using skinned breast reduces the fat significantly.

SERVES 2

1 hour 15 minutes

★

INGREDIENTS:

◆ 2 large (150–200g/5½–6½oz) boneless, skinned chicken breasts
◆ 15ml/1 tbsp olive oil
◆ 1 onion, chopped
◆ 2 garlic cloves, crushed
◆ 250g/8oz mushrooms, sliced
◆ 1 small bunch of fresh thyme or 1 tsp dried
◆ 2 tbsp flour
◆ salt and pepper
◆ 250ml/9fl oz red wine

METHOD:

Preheat the oven to 180°C/350°F/Gas Mark 4. In a medium frying pan, heat the oil and fry the onion and garlic for about 5 minutes until transparent and golden. Add the mushrooms and cook for 10 minutes (the juices should have evaporated). Spoon half this mixture into a small ovenproof dish and place the chicken and thyme on top, then sprinkle with the flour and salt and pepper. Cover with the remaining mushroom mixture and gently pour over the wine. Bake for 30–40 minutes until chicken is cooked through. As the coq au vin cooks, the alcohol will evaporate, leaving only the flavour of the red wine. Serve with rice or potatoes and steamed vegetables.

TURKEY KORMA WITH BEANS

SERVES 2

40 minutes

★

INGREDIENTS:

- ◆ *15ml/1 tbsp rapeseed oil or ghee*
- ◆ *330g/11oz turkey breast, sliced*
- ◆ *1 garlic clove, crushed*
- ◆ *1 onion, sliced*
- ◆ *4 tbsp korma paste*
- ◆ *400g/14oz tomatoes, chopped*
- ◆ *1 tbsp plain flour*
- ◆ *100g/3½oz low-fat fromage frais, or thick yogurt*
- ◆ *200g/6½oz green beans, sliced in 5cm/2 inch lengths*

METHOD:

Heat the oil in a medium pan or wok and quickly stir-fry the turkey for about 2 minutes. Remove and set aside, then add the onions and garlic to the pan. Cook for 3 minutes then add the korma paste, and cook for 2 minutes more. Sprinkle over the flour and cook for 1 minute, then add the tomatoes, cook for 10 minutes. Blanch the beans in boiling water for 3 minutes then drain and refresh under cold water. Stir the fromage frais or yogurt into the tomatoes with the turkey and heat gently for 5 minutes. Add the beans and cook for 2 more minutes. Serve with rice.

Dried beans, together with lentils and chickpeas, are collectively known as pulses. They are filling, inexpensive and high in protein and dietary fibre, but have gained a reputation for being bland and boring. This couldn't be further from the truth, with the hundreds of varieties available and different ways of serving them, there really is something for everyone.

As most beans react in the same way during cooking, it is possible to substitute varieties if one is unavailable, or if you feel like a change. When using dried beans, soak them overnight and then boil them rapidly for 10 minutes before you start cooking, to release the toxins. Changing the water after this process is thought to reduce the likelihood of gas after your bean meal!

AUBERGINE HOUMOUS

Aubergines give a twist to this popular spread. Although houmous is readily available, this home-made version is much lower in fat than shop-bought varieties.

SERVES 2

25 minutes

★★

INGREDIENTS:

- ◆ *250g/8oz aubergine*
- ◆ *1 garlic clove, crushed*
- ◆ *1 tsp cumin seeds*
- ◆ *5ml/1 tsp olive oil*
- ◆ *200g/6½oz cooked chickpeas*
- ◆ *30ml/2 tbsp tahini (optional)*
- ◆ *salt and pepper*
- ◆ *juice of 1 lemon*
- ◆ *15g/½oz fresh parsley or coriander, chopped*

METHOD:

Preheat the oven to 180°C/350°F/Gas Mark 4. Halve the aubergine lengthways and place skin side down in a roasting dish. Rub the cut side with the garlic and sprinkle with the cumin seeds and oil. Bake for 20 minutes until soft. Chop the aubergine roughly and place in a blender or food processor with the remaining ingredients. Blend, drizzling in enough water to form a soft purée.

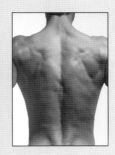

BEANS & RICE

This classic combination of a pulse with a grain, gives all the protein needed for a healthy diet, not to mention the fact it is filling and inexpensive. Dried beans should always be boiled rapidly for 10 minutes before cooking to release the toxins.

SERVES 2

1 hour 10 minutes

★

INGREDIENTS:

- *200g/6½oz dried kidney beans*
- *2 onions cut in wedges*
- *2 garlic cloves, sliced*
- *1 scotch bonnet chilli*
- *150g/5oz lean smoked ham, cubed*
- *7g/¼oz fresh thyme, tied in a bunch*
- *1 litre/1¾ pints chicken stock*
- *150g/5oz long grain white rice*
- *salt and pepper*

METHOD:

Cover the beans with 750ml/1¼ pints of water and soak overnight then drain. In a pan, bring the soaked beans to the boil and boil rapidly for 10 minutes. Drain again. Place the beans, ham, garlic, onion, chilli (leave whole) and thyme in a large pan and cover with the stock. Bring to the boil then reduce to a simmer and cook until tender, about 40 minutes. Remove the chilli and thyme, add the rice and a bit more water if necessary. Bring back to the boil and then simmer part covered until the rice is cooked, in about 15 minutes. Season with salt and pepper if necessary.

BUTTER & BROAD BEAN SOUP

If you add a whole fresh bunch of oregano to the beans it will flavour the soup while cooking and can easily be removed before eating.

SERVES 2

1 hour 30 minutes

★★

INGREDIENTS:

- ◆ *15ml / 1 tbsp olive oil*
- ◆ *2 small leeks, sliced*
- ◆ *200g / 6½oz dried butter beans, soaked overnight*
- ◆ *15g / ½oz fresh oregano or 10ml / 2 tsp dried*
- ◆ *2 cloves garlic*
- ◆ *1 litre / 1¾ pints chicken or vegetable stock*
- ◆ *200g / 6½oz broad beans, blanched or skinned*
- ◆ *juice of 1 lemon*
- ◆ *salt and pepper*

METHOD:

Drain and rinse the butter beans and place in a large pan covered with plenty of water. Bring to the boil and boil rapidly for 10 minutes, then drain. Heat the oil and gently sweat the leeks and garlic over a very low heat for 10 minutes. Add the butter beans, oregano and stock and bring to the boil. Simmer for 1 hour, topping up with water if required until the beans are starting to break up. Remove the oregano stalks. Stir in the broad beans, lemon juice and salt and pepper and cook for a further 5 minutes.

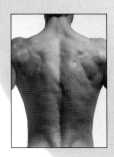

CORN & SWEET POTATO SOUP WITH BEANS

SERVES 2

50 minutes

★

INGREDIENTS:

- ◆ *15ml/1 tbsp rapeseed oil*
- ◆ *1 onion, finely chopped*
- ◆ *2 large sweet potatoes, peeled and chopped*
- ◆ *1 large potato, peeled and chopped*
- ◆ *1 litre/1¾ pints chicken or vegetable stock*
- ◆ *220g/7½oz tin of corn kernels, drained or the kernels taken from 2–3 cobs*
- ◆ *220g/7½oz cooked butter beans*
- ◆ *salt and pepper*

METHOD:

Heat the oil in a large saucepan and gently sweat the onion for about 10 minutes, it shouldn't go brown. Add the sweet potato, potatoes and the stock and bring to the boil, turn down the heat and cook for 20 minutes until potatoes are tender. Mash the potatoes in the saucepan or purée in a blender and then pour back into the pan. Add the corn and the beans and heat through, about 10 minutes. Season with salt and pepper. Serve with warm crusty bread.

COTTAGE PIE

This a meat-free version of traditional cottage pie but you could easily add 150g/5oz of lean mince after cooking the onions. Substitute any vegetables you like for the ones suggested here.

SERVES 4

50 minutes

★

INGREDIENTS:

- ◆ *15ml/1 tbsp rapeseed oil*
- ◆ *2 garlic cloves, crushed*
- ◆ *1 onion, chopped*
- ◆ *1 carrot, grated*
- ◆ *1 parsnip, grated*
- ◆ *1 courgette, grated*
- ◆ *100g/3½oz peas*
- ◆ *400g/14oz tinned tomatoes, chopped*
- ◆ *400g/14oz tin of brown lentils, drained*
- ◆ *5ml/1tsp tomato purée*
- ◆ *1 stock cube*
- ◆ *2 tsp mixed herbs*
- ◆ *200g/7oz mashed potato*
- ◆ *50g/2oz half-fat cheddar cheese, grated*

METHOD:

Preheat the oven to 180°C/350°F/Gas Mark 4. Heat the oil in a large pan and cook the garlic and onions for 3 minutes. Add the carrot parsnip, and courgette, then the peas, tomatoes, lentils, tomato purée, stock cube and mixed herbs. Stir and pour into a small casserole dish. Top with the mashed potato. Sprinkle with the cheese and bake for 40 minutes until golden brown.

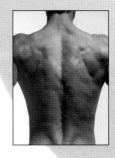

FALAFEL PATTIES

In order to cut out deep-frying, the usual way to cook falafel, I have added potato to the mixture to make it less crumbly.

SERVES 2

20 minutes

★★

INGREDIENTS:

- ◆ *400g/14oz cooked chickpeas*
- ◆ *2 garlic cloves*
- ◆ *4 shallots or spring onions, chopped finely*
- ◆ *15g/½oz fresh parsley, chopped*
- ◆ *1 tsp ground cumin*
- ◆ *1 tsp ground coriander*
- ◆ *1 tsp salt*
- ◆ *250g/8oz mashed potato*
- ◆ *30ml/2 tbsp olive oil*

METHOD:

Place the chickpeas in a food processor and blend, then add the remaining ingredients, half the oil, and process to a firm, smooth mixture. Shape into 16 patties. Heat the remaining oil in a large frying pan and cook the patties for about 4 minutes each side. Serve in pitta bread pockets with a selection of accompaniments such as tabouleh, shredded lettuce, tomato, cucumber and yogurt sauce, hot pepper sauce, tahini dressing.

MOROCCAN-STYLE CHICKPEAS WITH LAMB

SERVES 2

45 minutes

★★

INGREDIENTS:

- 15ml/1 tbsp rapeseed oil
- 150g/5oz lean lamb fillet, cubed
- 2 garlic cloves, crushed
- 1 onion, sliced
- 1 tsp ground cumin
- 2 tsp mild paprika
- 150g/5oz aubergine cut into 2cm/1 inch cubes
- 400g/14oz tin cooked chickpeas, drained
- 400g/14oz tin tomatoes, chopped
- juice of 1 lemon
- 15g/½oz fresh parsley or coriander, chopped
- 5–10ml/1–2 tsp harrisa paste, to serve (optional)

METHOD:

Heat the oil in a heavy-based saucepan or casserole. Quickly stir-fry the lamb for 2 minutes, then remove and set aside. Lower the heat, and cook the garlic, onion, cumin and paprika and aubergine for about 5 minutes. Stir in the tomatoes and bring to the boil. Reduce to a low simmer and add the chickpeas and lamb. Cover and cook gently for 30 minutes, then stir in the lemon juice, parsley or coriander and harrisa, if using. Serve over rice, couscous or potatoes.

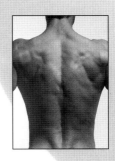

REAL MEN DO EAT QUICHE!

PASTA & BEAN SOUP

Flageolet beans are small, pale green and tender, but cannellini or butter beans work just as well.

SERVES 2
20 minutes
★

INGREDIENTS:

- 15ml/1 tbsp olive oil
- 1 garlic clove, crushed
- 1 medium onion, chopped
- 1 courgette, in small cubes
- 150g/5oz celeriac, in small cubes, or 2 celery stalks, sliced
- 100g/3½oz small pasta shapes (e.g. macaroni or orzo)
- 1 litre/1¾ pints chicken or vegetable stock
- 200g/7oz tin flageolet beans, drained
- salt and pepper
- 4 medium tomatoes, peeled, de-seeded and chopped
- 10g/⅓oz fresh parsley, chopped

METHOD:

Heat the oil in a medium pan. Gently cook the onions, garlic, courgette and celeriac for 5 minutes. Add the stock and bring to the boil. Add the pasta and cook for 5 minutes. Add the beans and cook a further 5 minutes then stir in the tomato and parsley and serve.

PEA & AVOCADO GUACAMOLE

A delicious variation of an old favourite. Bright green peas add colour and vitamins. Serve as a snack, or as a filling for baked potatoes to accompany grilled fish or chicken.

SERVES 2–4
10 minutes
★

INGREDIENTS:

- *125g/4½oz frozen peas*
- *1 small avocado, peeled and chopped*
- *1 garlic clove, crushed*
- *3 spring onions, chopped*
- *juice of 1 lemon*
- *1 red chilli, de-seeded and chopped (optional)*
- *salt and pepper*

METHOD:
Place the peas in a food processor and blend to a smooth purée. Add the remaining ingredients with salt and pepper to taste, and pulse until blended but not smooth. Serve with raw vegetables, toasted pitta bread or tortilla chips.

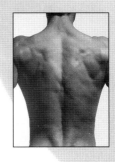

RE-FRIED BEAN TACOS

As a filling for tacos, kidney beans make a great alternative to meat. Re-frying cooked beans helps to develop their flavour.

SERVES 2
15 minutes
★

INGREDIENTS:

- *15ml/1 tbsp rapeseed oil*
- *1 onion, finely chopped*
- *400g/14oz tin kidney beans, drained*
- *200ml/7fl oz chicken or vegetable stock*
- *salt and pepper*
- *4–6 taco shells*
- *1 little gem lettuce, sliced*
- *1 red pepper, sliced*
- *100ml/3½fl oz tomato salsa*
- *sour cream, avocado and fresh coriander to serve (optional)*

METHOD:

Heat the oil in a medium-sized frying pan, add the onion and fry gently. Add about one-third of the beans, with a little stock, mashing and stirring as they cook. Continue adding the beans and stock, mashing together until you have a thick paste-like mixture. Season with salt and pepper. Continue cooking until the mixture is drying out around the edges. Pile into warmed taco shells with lettuce and pepper and topped with a spoonful of salsa. Serve with sour cream, avocado and coriander if using.

SPICY BLACK-EYED BEAN DIP

Bean dips are a great alternative to the cream-based dips usually served with vegetables and crisps. They are much creamier than a salsa and the beans make them more nutritious as well. Practically any bean can be substituted for the black-eyed variety.

SERVES 2

15 minutes

★

INGREDIENTS:

- 15ml/1 tbsp rapeseed oil
- 2 cloves garlic
- 1 red onion, chopped
- 1 tsp ground coriander
- 1 tsp ground cumin
- 1 tsp chilli powder (mild or hot, according to taste)
- 400g/14oz black-eyed beans, cooked
- 100ml/3½fl oz thick tomato juice or purée
- 15g/½oz fresh coriander, chopped
- 30ml/2 tbsp tomato paste
- 50g/2oz sour cream (optional)

METHOD:

Heat the oil in a medium saucepan and sauté the garlic, onions, coriander, cumin and chilli over a low heat for about 5 minutes. Add the beans and tomato juice. Add this with the fresh coriander, tomato paste and sour cream to a blender or food processor and blend to a rough purée. Serve with corn chips, pitta bread or vegetables.

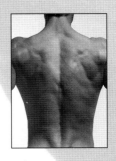

SPICY CAULIFLOWER WITH LENTILS & RICE

Cauliflower is perfect with these spicy lentils, which are cooked with the rice to give a great-flavoured filling meal.

SERVES 2

1 hour

★

INGREDIENTS:

- *100g/3½oz red lentils, washed*
- *750ml/1¼ pints chicken or vegetable stock*
- *1 garlic clove, crushed*
- *2cm/1 inch fresh ginger, grated*
- *1 tsp turmeric*
- *1 tsp salt (optional)*
- *100g/3½oz basmati or long grain rice*
- *200g/7oz cauliflower, in small florets*
- *2 tsp cumin seeds*
- *15ml/1 tbsp groundnut oil*

METHOD:

Bring the lentils to the boil in a large pan with the stock, skim then add the garlic, ginger and turmeric. Lower the heat and simmer for about 40 minutes, part-covered, stirring occasionally. Meanwhile, bring a medium pan of water to the boil and add the cauliflower. Cook for 1 minute then quickly drain and refresh with cold water. (This process is known as 'blanching'.) Add the salt, if needed, and rice to the lentils and cook for 10 more minutes before adding the cauliflower and cooking for a further 5 minutes. Heat the oil and cook the cumin seeds gently for 3 minutes. Add the oil and cumin to the mixture. Serve.

SPICY CHICKPEA POCKETS WITH TAHINI SAUCE

SERVES 2–4

15 minutes

★

INGREDIENTS:

- 15ml/1 tbsp oil
- 1 garlic clove, crushed
- 1 tbsp curry paste
- ½ tsp cumin seeds
- 1 aubergine, chopped
- 2 large tomatoes, peeled, de-seeded and chopped
- 400g/14oz tin chickpeas, drained
- 2 courgettes, chopped
- 4 pitta breads

TAHINI SAUCE:

- 90ml/6 tbsp tahini
- 150ml/5fl oz warm water
- juice of ½ a lemon

METHOD:

To make the tahini sauce, place the ingredients in a blender and blend until frothy, seasoning with salt and pepper. Any sauce not used can be stored in the fridge for up to two weeks.

Heat the oil and add the garlic, curry paste and cumin seeds, gently frying for 1 minute. Add the aubergine and cook, stirring occasionally, for a further 3 minutes. Add the courgettes, chickpeas and tomato and 3 tbsp of water. Heat through for about 5 minutes. Pile into warmed and split pitta breads and drizzle with tahini sauce.

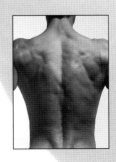

SPICY LENTIL SOUP

SERVES 4

1 hour

★

INGREDIENTS:

- ◆ *330g/11oz red lentils*
- ◆ *1.2 litres/2 pints chicken or vegetable stock*
- ◆ *2 garlic cloves, crushed*
- ◆ *3cm/1½ inch ginger, finely chopped*
- ◆ *1 tsp each, ground cumin, coriander and turmeric or 1 tbsp curry powder*
- ◆ *1 onion, finely chopped*
- ◆ *1 stick celery, finely chopped*
- ◆ *1 tsp mustard seeds (optional)*
- ◆ *15g/½ oz fresh coriander or parsley, chopped*
- ◆ *5ml/1 tsp groundnut oil*

METHOD:

Place the lentils and stock in a large saucepan and bring to the boil. Skim off any foam. Add the remaining ingredients, except the fresh coriander/parsley, the mustard seeds and the oil. Lower the heat to a steady simmer and cover. Cook for about 45 minutes to 1 hour, stirring occasionally, until lentils have broken to form a purée-like consistency. Add salt to taste. Heat 5ml/1 tsp of oil in a small pan and add the mustard seeds. Heat for about 2 minutes, until they pop. Serve the soup scattered with the coriander or parsley and the mustard seeds, and some warmed naan bread.

VEGETABLE
BURGERS

If you like a bit more kick in your burger, spice up the lentil mixture with a dash of Tabasco sauce and 1 tsp each of cumin and coriander.

MAKES 6

15 minutes

★

INGREDIENTS:

- ◆ *200g/6½oz cooked brown or green lentils*
- ◆ *1 garlic clove, crushed*
- ◆ *1 small onion, grated*
- ◆ *1 medium potato, boiled and mashed*
- ◆ *1 courgette, grated*
- ◆ *1 carrot, grated*
- ◆ *1 egg, lightly beaten*
- ◆ *100g/3½oz fresh wholemeal breadcrumbs*
- ◆ *3–6 burger buns*
- ◆ *15ml/1 tbsp oil*
- ◆ *selection of toppings (e.g. lettuce, tomatoes, beetroot, relish, ketchup, pickles)*
- ◆ *salt and pepper*

METHOD:

In a bowl, lightly mash the lentils. Stir in the next 6 ingredients and enough of the breadcrumbs to make a firm mixture. Season with salt and pepper. With wet hands, form into 6 patties. Heat the oil in a frying pan over a medium heat, and fry the patties gently, for about 8 minutes each side until golden and cooked through. Serve on one half of a bun. Top with toppings of choice and another half of bun, if using.

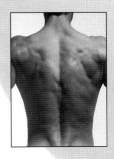

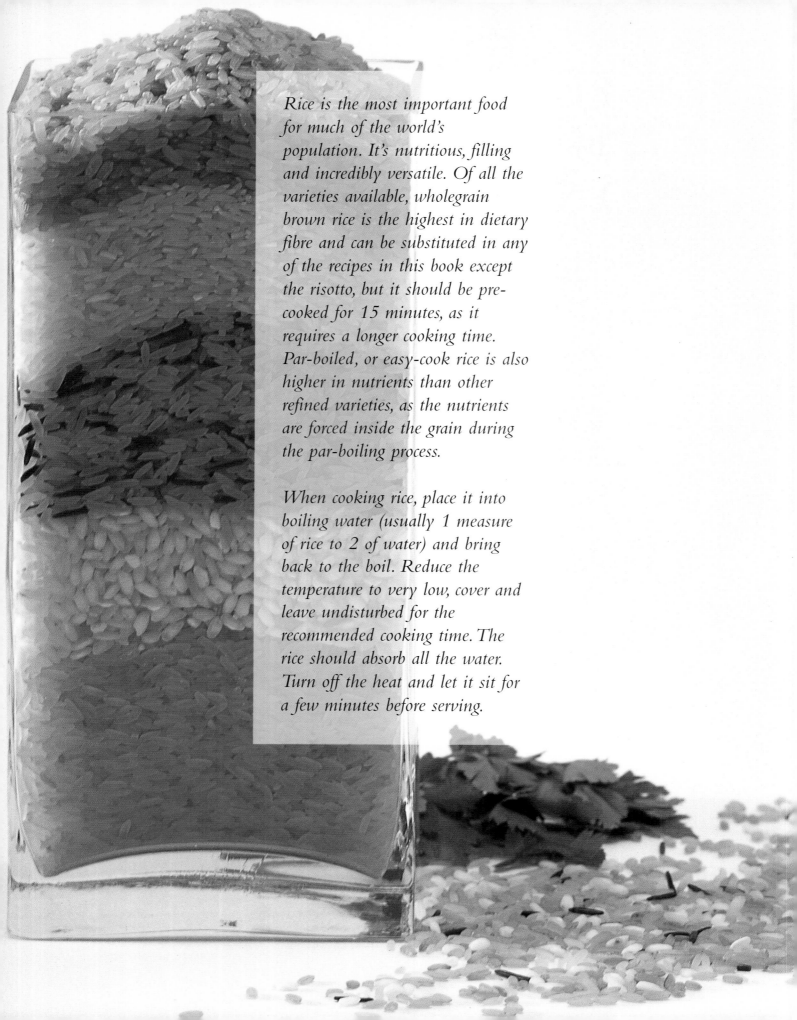

Rice is the most important food for much of the world's population. It's nutritious, filling and incredibly versatile. Of all the varieties available, wholegrain brown rice is the highest in dietary fibre and can be substituted in any of the recipes in this book except the risotto, but it should be pre-cooked for 15 minutes, as it requires a longer cooking time. Par-boiled, or easy-cook rice is also higher in nutrients than other refined varieties, as the nutrients are forced inside the grain during the par-boiling process.

When cooking rice, place it into boiling water (usually 1 measure of rice to 2 of water) and bring back to the boil. Reduce the temperature to very low, cover and leave undisturbed for the recommended cooking time. The rice should absorb all the water. Turn off the heat and let it sit for a few minutes before serving.

BAKED MUSHROOMS WITH BROWN RICE AND SPINACH

SERVES 2

40 minutes

★

INGREDIENTS:

- ◆ *15ml/1 tbsp of olive oil*
- ◆ *2 garlic cloves, crushed*
- ◆ *1 onion, finely chopped*
- ◆ *4 large flat mushrooms, stalks cut off, chopped and reserved*
- ◆ *175g/6oz cooked brown rice*
- ◆ *50g/1½oz walnuts, chopped, or whole pine kernels*
- ◆ *150g/5oz spinach*
- ◆ *50g/1½oz goat's cheese, grated*
- ◆ *salt and pepper*

METHOD:

Heat the oven to 180°C/350°F/Gas Mark 4. Heat the oil in a frying pan and cook the garlic, onion and mushroom stalks for 3 minutes. Add the rice and walnuts (or pine kernels) and salt and pepper as required. Place the mushrooms in a roasting dish and pile in the rice. Steam the spinach in 1cm/½ inch of boiling water until just wilted, about 1 minute. Cover the rice with the spinach and sprinkle with the cheese. Bake for about 30 minutes. Serve with salad for a light lunch or supper. Or, try with scrambled eggs and toast for a more substantial start to the day.

CABBAGE, POTATO & RICE SOUP

SERVES 2

30 minutes

★

INGREDIENTS:

- 15ml / 1 tbsp olive oil
- 2 garlic cloves, finely sliced
- 1 onion, sliced
- 2 tsp whole cumin seeds
- 50g / 1½oz long grain rice
- 1 large potato, peeled and cubed
- 200g / 6½oz cabbage, sliced
- 1 litre / 1¾ pints chicken or vegetable stock
- salt and pepper

METHOD:

Heat the oil in a large saucepan and sauté the garlic, onion, cumin and potato for about 5 minutes. Stir in the rice and cabbage and then the stock. Bring to the boil, then turn down to a simmer and cook for about 20 minutes. Season with salt and pepper and serve with crusty bread.

NUTTY PILAU RICE

SERVES 2

45 MINUTES

★

INGREDIENTS:

- 15ml / 1 tbsp olive oil
- 2 garlic cloves, crushed
- 1 onion, chopped
- 1 tsp ground cumin
- 1 tbsp paprika
- 200g / 6½oz long grain rice
- 450ml / 16fl oz chicken or vegetable stock
- 100g / 3½oz barley
- 15g / ½oz fresh parsley, chopped
- 50g / 1½oz toasted almonds, chopped

METHOD:

Heat the oil in a heavy-based pan or casserole and stir in the garlic and onions and cook for 5 minutes. Stir in the cumin and paprika, then the rice and barley and stir. Pour in the stock and bring to the boil, then reduce to a simmer. Cover and cook, undisturbed for 30 minutes on the lowest temperature possible. Stir in the parsley and the almonds and serve.

FRIED RICE

SERVES 2
★

INGREDIENTS:

- 250g/8oz cooked rice, cooled
- 15ml/1 tbsp groundnut oil
- 1 egg, beaten lightly
- 1 garlic clove, crushed
- 1 small onion, cut in wedges
- 300g/10oz of mixed vegetables (e.g. carrot, peppers, beans), cut into bite-sized pieces
- 200g/6½oz thin sliced ham or chicken, cut into strips
- 45ml/3 tbsp soya sauce
- 30ml/2 tbsp ketchup or tomato purée

METHOD:
Heat 5ml/1 tsp of the oil in a small frying pan and pour in the egg to make a thin omelette. It will be cooked almost immediately. Roll up the omelette and slice finely. Set aside. Heat the remaining oil in a large frying pan or wok. Add the garlic and onion and cook for 3 minutes. Add the remaining ingredients and stir-fry for 5 minutes, until vegetables are heated through but still a bit crunchy. Serve scattered with the omelette strips.

REAL MEN DO EAT QUICHE!

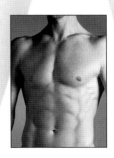

VEGETABLE RICE WITH EGGS

This works equally well with boiled and cubed potatoes for a change, like bubble and squeak.

SERVES 2

45 minutes

★

INGREDIENTS:

- 15ml/1 tbsp olive oil
- 300g/10oz cooked rice
- 6 spring onions, chopped
- 200g/6½oz green cabbage, chopped
- 2 carrots, grated
- 200g/6½oz broccoli, in small florets
- 2 sticks celery, sliced
- 100ml/3½fl oz chicken or vegetable stock
- 2.5ml/½ tsp Worcestershire sauce
- 2 eggs
- salt and pepper

METHOD:

Heat the oil in a large frying pan with a lid. Cover the base with the rice and then the vegetables. Season with salt and pepper and sprinkle on the stock and Worcestershire sauce to help steam the vegetables. Cover and cook for 10 minutes then crack the eggs on top and cover again for another 2–4 minutes, depending on how you like them. Alternatively, preheat the oven to 180°C/350°F/ Gas Mark 4 and place the rice and vegetables in a small baking dish and pour over the stock and Worcestershire sauce, with the salt and pepper. Cover and bake for 20 minutes. Preheat the grill, crack the eggs over the baked dish and grill for 2–4 minutes.

PEA & HAM RISOTTO

I think butter is an essential part of risotto, and if added at the end of the cooking, rather than the beginning, you need a lot less. That said, I have made it optional in this version, as the intense pea flavour disguises the lack of butter to a certain extent.

SERVES 2

30 minutes

★

INGREDIENTS:

- ◆ *15ml/1 tbsp olive oil*
- ◆ *250g/8oz arborio rice*
- ◆ *1 onion, finely chopped*
- ◆ *150ml/5fl oz white wine*
- ◆ *750ml/1¼ pints hot chicken or vegetable stock*
- ◆ *330g/11oz frozen peas*
- ◆ *150g/5oz ham, sliced or cubed*
- ◆ *25g/1oz butter (optional)*
- ◆ *mint to decorate*
- ◆ *salt and pepper*

METHOD:

Place half the peas in a blender or food processor and blend with about 50ml/2fl oz of the stock. Set aside. Heat the oil in a medium saucepan, add the onion and fry gently for 2–3 minutes. Add the rice and stir to coat. Pour in the wine and let it bubble. Add one quarter of the stock and cook over a gentle heat until it is nearly absorbed, about 6 minutes, then add one quarter more repeating the process until the stock is used up, stirring frequently. You should be left with thick soupy risotto; the rice should be firm but cooked through. Season with salt and pepper if necessary. Stir in all the peas and ham and heat through, about 3 minutes. Stir in the butter and serve sprinkled with the mint.

THAI SWEET POTATO & SPINACH CURRY

Thai curries are delicious made with almost any vegetable, but this combination of sweet potato and spinach works particularly well. Coconut cream makes this curry extra good, but is high in fat, so only a small amount is used.

SERVES 2

40 minutes

★★

THE CURRY PASTE:

- ◆ *30ml/2 tbsp groundnut oil*
- ◆ *10 shallots, peeled and chopped*
- ◆ *2 garlic cloves, crushed*
- ◆ *1–2 red chillies, de-seeded and chopped*
- ◆ *3cm/1½ inch fresh ginger, peeled and chopped*
- ◆ *2 stems of lemon grass, peeled and chopped*
- ◆ *1 bunch of coriander, roots and stems chopped leaves reserved*

THE CURRY:

- ◆ *2 large sweet potatoes, chopped into 2cm/1 inch cubes*
- ◆ *1 large potato, chopped into 2cm/1 inch cubes*
- ◆ *500ml/18fl oz chicken or vegetable stock*
- ◆ *200ml/6½fl oz coconut milk*
- ◆ *225g/7½oz spinach, washed*
- ◆ *salt*

METHOD:

Place the curry paste ingredients in a blender or food processor and process into a paste, adding more oil if necessary (alternatively crush with a large pestle and mortar). Heat a wok or large saucepan and add 45–60ml/3–4 tbsps of the curry paste with the sweet potato, potato and stir-fry for 3 minutes (if it sticks add a little of the stock).

Add the stock and simmer part covered for 20 minutes until potatoes are tender. Stir in the coconut milk and salt to taste and bring back to simmer. Stir in the spinach and cook for 1 more minute. Serve with rice or noodles and sprinkle with the remaining coriander.

(Any leftover paste can be stored in the fridge for 2 weeks. If time or ingredients are short, substitute any store-bought red Thai curry paste.)

THREE-GRAIN TABOULEH

Tabouleh is a Middle Eastern salad, consisting mainly of parsley and bulgar wheat. In this version, the increased quantity of grains gives a less sharp, more wholesome salad, but still with the traditional favour.

SERVES 2
1 hour 10 minutes
★

INGREDIENTS:

- 170g/6oz cooked bulgar wheat
- 200g/6½oz cooked barley
- 200g/6½oz cooked couscous
- juice of 2 lemons
- 2 garlic cloves, crushed
- 1 cup fresh parsley, chopped
- 4 spring onions, chopped
- 30ml/2 tbsp olive oil
- 1 tbsp fresh mint (optional)
- 2 tomatoes, de-seeded and chopped

METHOD:

Combine the cooked grains with the remaining ingredients in a large bowl. Cover and refrigerate for at least 1 hour before serving.

Few meals are complete without vegetables, and some consist entirely of them. Vegetables are packed with vitamins and minerals, as well as being valuable sources of carbohydrate and fibre. This section contains some hard-core vegetable recipes.

To get the most out of your vegetables, cook them quickly using methods such as steaming, stir-frying or microwaving. Remember to use a variety of seasonal produce — the list of what's available is endless — as different vegetables contain different vitamins and minerals.

GAZPACHO

Gazpacho is an amazing soup! Not only is it beautifully colourful and incredibly easy to make, but it is also full of vitamins. Peppers can be peeled with a vegetable peeler to retain maximum vitamins and freshness, or they can be halved and grilled, skin side up, until very black, then the black skin can be peeled off.

SERVES 4

15 minutes

★

INGREDIENTS:

- *2 slices of bread, cubed*
- *600ml/1 pint tomato juice*
- *2 yellow or orange peppers, peeled, de-seeded and chopped*
- *750g/1lb 10oz tomatoes, peeled, de-seeded and chopped*
- *2 cloves of garlic, crushed*
- *30ml/2 tbsp olive oil*
- *30ml/2 tbsp sherry or white wine vinegar*
- *salt and pepper*
- *4 spring onions, diagonally sliced*
- *½ cucumber*

METHOD:

Place the bread, 300ml/11fl oz of juice, peppers, tomatoes and garlic into a food processor or blender and blend until a coarse purée is formed. If the blender/ processor bowl is big enough, add the oil, sherry, salt and pepper and remaining juice and blend until combined. Alternatively, pour the mixture into a bowl and combine by hand. Halve the cucumber lengthways and slice on the diagonal quite finely. Serve the gazpacho with cucumber and spring onions.

CARROT, MUSHROOM & NUT LOAF

A good warming meal. Serve like meat loaf with peas and potatoes. If you are worried about cholesterol, use egg whites instead of whole eggs.

SERVES 4
50 minutes
★★

INGREDIENTS:

- 1 onion, finely chopped
- 30g/1oz butter
- 4 tbsp plain flour
- 150ml/5fl oz skimmed milk
- 2 eggs or 4 egg whites
- 250g/8oz mushrooms, chopped
- 2 medium carrots, grated
- 45ml/3tbsp water
- 50g/1½oz walnuts, chopped
- 15g/½oz fresh parsley, chopped
- salt and pepper

METHOD:

Preheat the oven to 180°C/350°F/Gas Mark 4. Oil and base line a small loaf tin with greaseproof or baking paper. Melt the butter in a small pan and stir in the flour and cook for 2 minutes then stir in the milk. Cook for about 3 minutes until thick. Cool slightly and beat in the eggs or egg whites. In a medium frying pan, heat 45ml/3 tbsp of water and cook the onion and mushrooms for 5 minutes. Season with salt and pepper, stir in the carrots, walnuts and parsley. Mix this with the white sauce and press into the loaf pan. Bake for 40 minutes until firm. Cool slightly then turn out and slice.

MUSHROOM & WALNUT STROGANOFF

SERVES 2

30 minutes

★

INGREDIENTS:

- ◆ *15ml/1 tbsp olive oil*
- ◆ *1 onion, sliced*
- ◆ *2 garlic cloves, crushed*
- ◆ *1 tbsp mild paprika*
- ◆ *330g/11oz mixed mushrooms (e.g. field, chestnut, horse), chopped*
- ◆ *1 tbsp flour*
- ◆ *1 tsp salt*
- ◆ *400ml/14fl oz vegetable stock*
- ◆ *100g/3½oz walnut pieces, toasted*
- ◆ *50ml/1½ fl oz low fat sour cream*
- ◆ *1 tbsp parsley, chopped*

METHOD:

Heat the oil in a large saucepan and fry the onion and garlic for 3 minutes. Add the paprika and cook for a further 2 minutes. Stir in the mushrooms and salt and cook for 5 minutes, then stir in the flour and cook for 1 minute. Pour in the stock and bring to the boil, then simmer for 15 minutes. Finely chop or grind the walnuts and add to the mushrooms with the sour cream and heat through. Stir in the parsley and serve over linguine, egg noodles or rice.

REAL MEN DO EAT QUICHE!

GREEK STUFFED PEPPERS

Peppers make a very colourful container for this delicious Greek-style stuffing, but other vegetables could be substituted, e.g. aubergine, large courgettes and tomatoes.

SERVES 2

45 minutes

★

INGREDIENTS:

- 1 red, 1 yellow and 1 green pepper
- 1½ cups cooked rice
- 200g/6½oz feta cheese, cubed
- 12–16 cherry tomatoes, halved
- 1 tbsp fresh oregano, chopped or ½ tbsp dried oregano
- ½ tsp salt
- 15ml/1 tbsp olive oil
- 12 black olives, halved and stones removed (optional)

METHOD:

Preheat oven to 180°C/350°F/Gas Mark 4. Halve the peppers lengthways, retaining their stalks and pepper shape. Remove and discard the seeds. Place in a baking dish. Combine the remaining ingredients except the oil in a bowl and pile into the peppers. Drizzle with the oil. Place in the oven and cook for 30–40 minutes. Serve with pitta or crusty bread.

SPICY TOFU WITH CORN

Tofu is an ingredient many people have had negative experiences with because of its bland taste... a disadvantage in itself but a distinct advantage when cooked with other strong flavours as it soaks them right up.

SERVES 2
25 minutes
★★

INGREDIENTS:
- *330g/11oz firm tofu, drained and cut into 1cm/½ inch cubes*
- *30ml/2 tbsp soy sauce*
- *15ml/1 tbsp clear honey*
- *15ml/1 tbsp chilli sauce*
- *15ml/1 tbsp rice, sherry or white wine vinegar*
- *30ml/2 tbsp groundnut oil*
- *4 spring onions, sliced diagonally*
- *2 garlic cloves, crushed*
- *3cm/1½ inch piece fresh ginger, shredded*
- *250g/8oz baby corn, with the ends trimmed off*
- *15ml/1 tbsp yellow bean sauce*
- *1 tsp cornflour, mixed with 15ml/1 tbsp of water* ◆
- *toasted sesame seeds (optional)*

METHOD:
Combine together the soy sauce, honey, chilli and vinegar in a bowl and stir in the tofu. Leave to marinate for 15 minutes. Heat the oil in a wok or frying pan and stir-fry the spring onions, garlic, ginger and corn for about 3 minutes. Add the tofu and marinade with the yellow bean sauce, then stir in the cornflour with about 15ml/1fl oz of water to make a sauce. Cook for 1 minute and serve over noodles or rice, sprinkled with the sesame seeds.

◆ Cornflour needs to be mixed or 'slackened' with a small amount of water before it is combined with other ingredients to prevent it from forming lumps.

ROAST VEGETABLE SALAD

Grilling and baking vegetables brings out all their wonderful flavours and often makes them seem more appetising to someone who finds the taste of steamed vegetables a little too raw for their liking.

SERVES 2

35 minutes

★

INGREDIENTS:

- 1 red onion cut into wedges
- 1 large fennel bulb, cut lengthways into 4
- 1 courgette, halved and cut lengthways into 2
- 1 pepper, de-seeded and cut into 4
- 1 small aubergine cut into quarters
- 2 garlic cloves, crushed
- 30ml/2 tbsp olive oil
- 1 tsp salt and pepper
- 15ml/1 tbsp balsamic vinegar or red wine vinegar

METHOD:

Preheat oven to 180°C/350°F/Gas Mark 4. Arrange the vegetables in a roasting dish. Mix the garlic, oil, salt and pepper together and pour over the vegetables. Stir to ensure the vegetables are coated. Bake for 30 minutes. Drizzle with the vinegar and stir to coat the vegetables in the vinegar and pan juices. Serve as an accompaniment to fish, chicken or meat. Or, try with couscous, pasta or a baked potato as a satisfying meal in itself.

VEGETABLE KEBABS WITH HALLOUMI CHEESE

MAKES 8

45 minutes

★

INGREDIENTS:

- *2 red onions, cut into 16 wedges*
- *2 medium courgettes cut into 16 pieces*
- *1 red pepper cut into 16 chunks*
- *16 small button or chestnut mushrooms*
- *16 large cherry tomatoes*
- *150g/5oz Halloumi cheese, cut into 24 pieces*

THE MARINADE:

- *30ml/2 tbsp olive oil*
- *15ml/1 tbsp vinegar (preferably balsamic)*
- *30ml/2 tbsp clear honey*
- *2 garlic cloves crushed*
- *15ml/1 tbsp lemon juice*
- *30ml/2 tbsp tomato purée or ketchup*
- *½ tsp salt*

METHOD:

Soak 8 wooden skewers in water for 30 minutes. Combine the marinade ingredients. Thread the vegetables and cheese onto the skewers (2 of each vegetable, 3 pieces of cheese per skewer). Place in a flat non-metal dish and pour on the marinade. Leave until ready to use, turning occasionally (at least 30 minutes, not more than 2 hours). Place kebabs on a preheated barbecue or

under a grill and cook for 8 minutes, turning once, until vegetables are brown and tender. Serve with a bulgar wheat salad, rice or the Three-Grain Tabouleh on page 83.

TOFU WITH BROCCOLI & PORK

This is a classic and very tasty combination, and the tofu bumps up the amount of protein without adding extra saturated fat.

SERVES 2
15 minutes
★

INGREDIENTS:

- 15ml/1 tbsp groundnut oil
- 4 spring onions, sliced
- 2 garlic cloves, crushed
- 100g/3 1/2oz lean pork mince
- 200g/6 1/2oz firm tofu, drained, patted dry and cut into 2cm/1 inch cubes
- 250g/8oz broccoli, in bite-sized pieces
- 30ml/2 tbsp soy sauce
- 15ml/1 tbsp white wine or rice vinegar
- 1 tbsp sugar
- 30ml/2 tbsp hoisin sauce

WATERCRESS & SPINACH SOUP WITH ALMONDS

Both watercress and spinach are amazingly high in iron, fibre and vitamins.

SERVES 2

45 minutes

★

INGREDIENTS:

- ◆ *15ml/1 tbsp olive oil*
- ◆ *2 garlic cloves, crushed*
- ◆ *2 small leeks, sliced*
- ◆ *1 medium potato, cubed*
- ◆ *450ml/16fl oz chicken or vegetable stock*
- ◆ *250ml/9fl oz skimmed milk*
- ◆ *85g/3oz watercress, chopped*
- ◆ *110g/4oz spinach, chopped*
- ◆ *salt and pepper*
- ◆ *50g/1½oz flaked almonds, toasted*

METHOD:
Heat the oil in a large pan and sauté the garlic and leeks gently over a low heat for 15 minutes, they should not go brown. Stir in the potato and then the stock and bring to the boil. Reduce to a simmer, season and cook until the potatoes are tender, about 15 minutes. Add the milk and bring almost to the boil. Stir in the watercress and spinach and take off the heat. Cool for 5–10 minutes to make it easier to handle, then blend to a creamy consistency. Re-heat gently. Serve scattered with the toasted almonds.

INDEX

A
almonds 14, 57, 78, 93
anchovies 18, 29, 46
apricots 49
artichokes 28
asparagus 52
aubergines 61, 67, 73, 90
avocado 24, 32, 46, 48, 49, 69, 70

B
bean sauce, yellow 89
beans,
    black-eyed 32, 71
    broad 63
    butter 27, 63, 64
    cannellini 12
    flageolet 68
    kidney 62, 70
    refried 70
    string 18
bulgar wheat 83

C
cannelloni 27
carrots 12, 17, 25, 31, 37, 41, 45, 47, 65, 75, 86
cauliflower 37, 72
celeriac 68
cheese,
    cheddar 12, 37, 65
    cottage 34, 40
    feta 42, 88
    goat's 37, 77
    halloumi 91
    Parmesan 27, 30, 33, 34, 35, 39, 40, 46

chestnuts, water 51
chicken 29, 45, 46, 47, 48, 50, 51, 52, 53, 54, 55, 56, 58, 80
chickpeas 15, 61, 66, 67, 73
chilli 10, 11, 15, 24, 25, 32, 51, 54, 62, 69, 82, 89
coconut 17, 82
courgettes 14, 50, 65, 68, 73, 75, 90, 91
couscous 83
cucumber 18, 85

D E
eggs 20, 22, 31, 35, 53, 75, 79, 80, 86

F
fennel 90
fish 8–12
focaccia 35
fromage frais 20, 59

G
garlic 12, 16, 17, 18, 19, 22, 24, 27, 28, 30, 32, 34, 37, 40, 41, 42, 59, 61, 62, 63, 65, 66, 67, 68, 69, 71, 72, 73, 74, 75, 77, 78, 79, 82, 83, 85, 89, 90, 91, 92, 93
ginger 24, 51, 65, 74, 82, 89
gnocchi 35

H I J
haddock 9, 12, 20
ham 62, 79, 81

K L
lamb 67

leek 27, 43, 47, 63, 93
lemon grass 24, 82
lentils 65, 72, 74, 75

M N
mackerel 21
mushrooms 28, 40, 58, 77, 87, 91
mussels 11, 16, 19
noodles 16, 41, 50, 56

O
oil,
    groundnut 10, 17, 24, 41, 50, 51,
    72, 74, 77, 78, 79, 81, 82, 92
    olive 9, 11, 12, 14, 15, 18, 23, 29,
    30, 31, 33, 34, 36, 37, 39, 40, 43,
    49, 52, 55, 57, 58, 83, 85, 87, 88,
    90, 91, 93
    rapeseed 19, 21, 22, 48, 59, 61, 63,
    64, 65, 66, 67, 68, 70
    vegetable 20, 75

P
Parmesan 27, 30, 33, 34, 35, 39, 40, 46
parsnips 30, 43, 65
pasta 26–43, 68
peas 12, 65, 69, 81
peppers 14, 19, 25, 41, 42, 48, 55, 85,
88, 90, 91
pesto 13
pineapple 25
pork 92
poultry 44–59
prawns 11, 19
pulses 60–75
pumpkin 35, 38

R S
rice 53, 62, 72
salmon 13
sole 23
spaghetti 37
spinach 30, 35, 39, 40, 77, 82, 93
squid 24
sweet potato 64, 82

T
Thai fish sauce 24
tofu 89, 92
tomatoes 11, 14, 18, 27, 29, 32, 37, 39,
40, 48, 55, 59, 65, 67, 68, 73, 83, 85,
88, 91
tuna 12, 39
turkey 56, 59

U V W
walnuts 28, 33, 57, 77, 86, 87
wine,
    red 58
    white 11, 16, 81

X Y Z
yogurt 56, 59